# The Charlottesville Collection

# The Charlottesville Collection

## Recipes from Jefferson Country

Volume 2

*June Peterson Oakley*

June Peterson Oakley

**HOWELL PRESS**

Charlottesville, Virginia

Designed by Carolyn Weary Brandt
Edited by Meghan M. Mitchell

Quotations and anecdotal material
pertaining to Charlottesville and
Albemarle County were drawn from the
collection of the Albemarle County
Historical Society. The image on page xiv
is reproduced with the permission of
Special Collections, University of Virginia,
and courtesy of the Albemarle County
Historical Society.

Library of Congress Catalog Card
    Number 99-96974
ISBN 1-57427-107-5
Printed in Canada
08  07  06  05  04  03  02  01  00  99

10  9  8  7  6  5  4  3  2  1

Published by Howell Press, Inc.
1713-2D Allied Lane
Charlottesville, VA  22903
(804) 977-4006
http://www.howellpress.com

# TABLE OF CONTENTS

# FOREWORD

Thomas Jefferson has been called the father of the American gastronomic revolution and our nation's first gourmet. In many ways, this reputation is well deserved. As president, he spent nearly one-third of his annual salary on food and drink. Even in his declining years, with dwindling financial resources, Jefferson's wine orders averaged about six hundred bottles per year.

The essence of Jefferson the connoisseur is deeply rooted in the red clay earth of Monticello's vegetable garden and the sun-kissed sweetness of its orchards. *The Charlottesville Collection: Recipes from Jefferson Country* reflects Jefferson's love for fine ingredients, a love born in the lush mountains of Albemarle County, Virginia, and nurtured in the capitals of Europe.

Indeed, the marriage of Virginia-grown ingredients with state-of-the art French culinary technology best characterizes Jefferson's contribution to American cuisine. His contemporaries recognized his table's hallmark blend of the best from the Old World and the New; in his memoirs, Daniel Webster noted that meals at Monticello were served in "half-Virginian, half-French style, in abundance and good taste." Margaret Bayard Smith, a Washington socialite who kept a detailed journal, described Jefferson's palate as "republican simplicity . . . united to Epicurean delicacy."[1]

While Jefferson's early culinary activities were undoubtedly influenced by his interests in gardening, agriculture, and technology, as well as his temperament, his travels in Europe left an indelible mark on his developing taste. His diplomatic service as ambassador to France brought him into contact with a variety of exciting ingredients that he investigated with relish and carried with him across the Atlantic. He learned that the best "maccaroni" in Italy was made with "a particular sort of flour called Semola" and ordered a pasta mold. He smuggled a small parcel of rice out of Lombardy, an offense punishable by death. After eating waffles in Holland, he purchased a waffle iron.

While in Europe, Jefferson also enthusiastically cultivated his knowledge of wine.

1. Merrill D. Peterson, ed., *Visitors to Monticello* (Charlottesville, Va.: Univ. of Virginia Press, 1989), 45-54, 97-99.

After sampling the wares of such distinguished houses as Châteaux Margaux and Hermitage, his tastes shifted away from fortified wines like Madeira toward Champagnes and the lighter wines of southern France and Italy. Despite his inclination for the wines of the Continent, however, Jefferson retained a fondness for those made from the humble Scuppernong grape, indigenous to North Carolina and Virginia.

As a result of Jefferson's tastes and travels, meals at Monticello during his retirement combined the refined flavors of European cuisine with the robust plentitude of the Virginia landscape. Most ingredients were plantation-grown, although such specialty items as anchovies, Maille mustard, vanilla beans, olive oil, chocolate, and capers were imported. Monticello's cellars were richly stocked with crackers, rice, sugar, tea, and coffee beans imported from the East and West Indies. Other imported provisions included Parmesan, Swiss, Stilton, and Gloucester cheese.

Jefferson took particular advantage of a local economy known internationally for its superior ham. One French visitor to Virginia noted, "The people here have a special way of curing [ham] that consists of salting and smoking them . . . almost as we do in France; however, ours cannot touch theirs for flavor and quality."[2] On an annual basis, Jefferson's family and guests consumed over three hundred hams. Because his farms could not always meet the demand, he sometimes purchased the meat from Smithfield and Hanover, as well as from Meriwether Lewis's aunt, Mary Walker Lewis.

Virginia's moderate climate and long growing season allowed Jefferson to grow more than 250 varieties of seventy different vegetables and 130 varieties of fruit trees. His favorite vegetable was the pea, and he proudly cultivated twenty-three different kinds. The garden included many exotic and experimental plants, such as the Jerusalem artichoke and Mexican pepper. Jefferson grew asparagus, tomatoes, eggplant, broccoli, cauliflower, squash, and several types of beans. The garden also reflected his preference for greens, including lettuce, endive, spinach, and nasturtiums. Each season offered distinct pleasures for gardener and gourmand.

The orchards provided equally bounteous gifts, which Jefferson called "precious refreshment." He cultivated apples like the Newtown Pippin, valued as a dessert fruit, and the Taliaferro, considered superior for cider production. Apricots, plums, cherries,

2. Jane Carson, *Colonial Virginia Cookery* (Williamsburg, Va.: The Colonial Williamsburg Foundation, 1967), 73.

strawberries, and raspberries also flourished, but for sheer abundance nothing surpassed the peach. Jefferson planted as many as thirty-eight varieties and delighted in "the luxury of the peach."

The richness and variety of produce from Monticello's garden and orchards enabled the household to set a fine table throughout the winter. Fruits and vegetables could be preserved in a number of ways. They could be pickled and brandied, salted and dried, or made into jellies and catsups. Instructions for these activities are found in period cookbooks, and Monticello's library included *The Art of Cookery Made Plain and Easy*, by Hannah Glasse, *La Cuisinière Bourgeoise*, by Menon, and *The Virginia House-wife*, by Mary Randolph. During his travels, Jefferson copied a number of recipes himself, including directions for making ice cream, blancmange, and macaroni.

For a widower with demanding social obligations and an insatiable appetite for fine food and drink, the talents of a trusted cook were especially important. Jefferson took his slave James Hemings to Paris, where he studied the art of cookery and eventually achieved the rank of *chef de cuisine*. Beginning with Hemings, all the slaves who were Monticello's cooks received training in the French culinary arts. They worked their magic on fine Virginia produce and imported delicacies with the help of a complete *batterie de cuisine*, including tin-lined copper pots, sauté pans and sauce-pans, and a variety of other state-of-the-art gadgets.

Indeed, under the direction of Jefferson's daughter, Martha Randolph, an entire staff of talented slaves, including cooks, butlers, and other servants, produced the sophisticated cuisine that made Monticello's hospitality a legend. As the clock in the Entrance Hall struck eight, guests might have enjoyed a hearty breakfast of muffins, cold ham, bacon, fried apples, and eggs. In the late afternoon, a sumptuous dinner might feature roast duck, *boeuf à la mode*, okra soup, peas, and apple fritters, accompanied by plantation-brewed cider or beer. A course of rich desserts, including ice cream, pies, crème brûlée, meringues, and jellies would follow. Then, with the sun setting behind Brown's Mountain and in the glitter of candlelight, the meal would come to an end with nuts, fruit, and a special wine selected by Mr. Jefferson.

Through his culinary exploration, Thomas Jefferson did America a great service by introducing a variety of plants, foods, and recipes to the gentry who had the pleasure of dining in his company. His research and educated palate added new dimensions and flavors to Southern cooking. The contributors to this collection have inherited this tradition and made it their own. Their innovative use of fresh ingredients from the magnificent farmlands of Virginia's Piedmont is combined with a bold sense of experimentation.

We hope you enjoy these recipes, which bring together the taste and traditions of the old and new South. Each proclaims the spirit of Epicurean adventure that is Jefferson's culinary legacy. It's a legacy we are delighted to share with you.

**Katherine Gratto Revell**

*As the first Gilder Fellow at the International Center for Jefferson Studies, a joint venture between the University of Virginia and the Thomas Jefferson Memorial Foundation, Ms. Revell researched domestic life at Monticello and produced a plan to refurnish and reinterpret the plantation's kitchen and related dependencies. She has ten years of experience working as a researcher and curator for Monticello, the Phillips Collection, the Munson-Williams-Proctor Institute, and the Atlanta College of Art.*

# PREFACE

The first volume of *The Charlottesville Collection* was a compilation of my friends' and relatives' recipes, restaurants' recipes, and recipes that had sustained me through forty years of cooking. Always a gardener and sometimes a farmer, I like to start from scratch and use fresh, homegrown ingredients. No dish can be better than its ingredients, so start with the best you can find and afford. Many years spent near the ocean have given me an appreciation for really fresh fish, so even today I return from a visit to my New Jersey cottage with a month's supply of fresh fish packed in ice.

My herb garden is another source of flavor. As I look at it today, I find that it has changed quite a bit in four years. Now I grow garlic cloves as well as the standard variety. Rocket (arugula), which I learned about in England, adds more zip to my salads. Shallots grow better in Charlottesville's clay soil than onions. Lemon thyme and chocolate mint have added new flavors.

The restaurant recipes in the first volume of *The Charlottesville Collection* were such a success that more restaurants asked to be included. Meanwhile, many friends and even some strangers gave me marvelous recipes, and so this second volume began. I hope you find it as helpful as the first. I have included more and different tips and shortcuts and some slightly fancier recipes. I'm a basic cook, not a gourmet cook, but the wide variety of ingredients available today makes it a challenge and a delight to try new things. If only time to fuss in the kitchen weren't so hard to come by!

In compiling this cookbook I feel I have increased the variety of foods I can offer my family with confidence. I hope it will enable you to do the same.

**June Peterson Oakley**

# ACKNOWLEDGMENTS

The recipes in this book have come from the kitchens of Charlottesville and the surrounding towns. Some are family recipes handed down through generations; others were developed with this book in mind. Many are for dishes that are favorites with entire families. The restaurants in town have generously contributed recipes for some of their best fare, making this a true Charlottesville Collection.

Some contributors have helped with the testing; some with the tasting or editing. Special thanks to Mark Levisay for his extensive testing and to Clairiece Humphrey, a regular contributor to *Southern Living*, for her special recipes.

The staff at Howell Press has had to work hard to form my recipes into an appealing book, and I am most grateful for everyone's patience and perseverance. I change my mind often and am apt to make last-minute changes in a recipe I thought was the best it could be.

Much thanks to all who contributed to this book, including:

| | | |
|---|---|---|
| Dan Aldrich | June E. Harris | Patt Oakley |
| Jean Aldrich | Clairiece Humphrey | Chris Oakley |
| Christine Baker | Doris Kellar | Betty Pasternak |
| Jack Bertram | Evelyn Kelskey | Joseph Pasternak |
| Susan Bertram | Dee Kennedy | Laurent Pedamy |
| Edie Brann | Mark Kennedy | Rachel Leigh Preston |
| Sandra Bruglio | Joan Klimm | Christa Rounds |
| Melanie R. Carratt | Barbara Levisay | Virginia Roy |
| Carol Betz Chambers | Mark Levisay | Sandy Russell |
| Doris Coon | Blaise MacInnis | Alda Sedlmayr |
| Sarah Dessert | Sandra Mueller | Katherine Sherman |
| Lorraine Diamond | Ann Nelson | Karen Sprague |
| Dorrie Drecht | Newcomer's Lunch Bunch | Betty Lou Stroh |

Special gratitude is owed to the following restaurants and chefs, who generously shared their recipes:

Boar's Head Inn
Ken Harnad, Director of Food
    and Beverage
200 Ednam Drive
Charlottesville, VA  22903
(804) 972-2230

BRIX Marketplace
Karen Laetare, Chef/Owner
1330 Thomas Jefferson Parkway
Charlottesville, VA  22902
(804) 295-7000

Caffe Bocce
Marcia I. Miller, Chef
330 Valley Street
Scottsville, VA  24590
(804) 286-4422

Clifton, The Country Inn
Rachel Greenberg, Executive Chef
1296 Clifton Inn Drive
Charlottesville, VA  22911
(804) 971-1800

Copper Mine Restaurant
Wintergreen Resort
Michael Miles, Chef
PO Box 706
Wintergreen, VA  22958
(804) 325-8090

Devils Grill Restaurant
Wintergreen Resort
Aaron Fultz, Chef
PO Box 706
Wintergreen, VA  22958
(804) 325-8100

The Edge at Cooper's Vantage Restaurant
Wintergreen Resort
David Hayden, Chef
PO Box 706
Wintergreen, VA  22958
(804) 325-8080

Hamiltons' at First & Main
Bill Hamilton, Certified Executive Chef
101 West Main Street
Charlottesville, VA  22902
(804) 295-6649

High Meadows Inn
David J. Barbieri, Chef
55 High Meadows Lane
Scottsville, VA  24590
(804) 286-2218

Ivy Inn
Angelo Vangelopoulos, Chef
2244 Old Ivy Road
Charlottesville, VA  22903
(804) 977-1222

Maharaja Indian Restaurant
Arun Durve, Chef
Seminole Square
Charlottesville, VA  22901
(804) 973-8444

The Nook Restaurant
Terry Shotwell, Owner
415 East Main Street
Charlottesville, VA  22902
(804) 295-6665

Northern Exposure
Stuart L. Rifkin, Owner
1202 West Main Street
Charlottesville, VA 22903
(804) 977-6002

The Ordinary at Michie Tavern,
    Circa 1784
683 Thomas Jefferson Parkway
Charlottesville, VA 22902
(804) 977-1234

Pizza Bella
Chris Manning, Owner
Hernan Franco, Head Chef
32 Millcreek Parkway
Southside Shopping Center,
    on Avon Street Extended
Charlottesville, VA 22901
(804) 296-7472

Prospect Hill, The Virginia
    Plantation Inn
The Sheehan Family, Innkeepers
2887 Poindexter Road
Trevilians, VA 23093
(800) 277-0844

Rococo's
Stuart L. Rifkin, Owner
2001 Commonwealth Drive
Charlottesville, VA 22901
(804) 971-7371

Schnitzelhouse Restaurant
Claire and Ed Gisler, Owners
2208 Fontaine Avenue
Charlottesville, VA 22903
(804) 293-7185

The St. Maarten Café
James S. Roland II, Owner
Michael M. L. Merritt, Sous Chef
1400 Wertland Street
Charlottesville, VA 22901
(804) 293-2233

Sweetbones
Peter A. Murphy, Chef and Owner
532 Pantops Center
Charlottesville, VA 22911
(804) 977-1020

Tastings of Charlottesville
Bill Curtis, Chef/Owner
502 East Market Street
Charlottesville, VA 22902
(804) 293-3663

The Tea Room Cafe at Starr Hill
Vickie and Mark Gresge, Proprietors
817 West Main Street
Charlottesville, VA 22903
(804) 979-7957

*A late-nineteenth-century view of
Main Street from Vinegar Hill.*

# ABOUT CHARLOTTESVILLE

Charlottesville has had a reputation for hospitality and conviviality since its establishment in 1762 by an act of the Virginia General Assembly. Created specifically to be the county seat of Albemarle County, it was named in honor of King George III's young bride, Queen Charlotte. A courthouse, jail, pillory, and whipping post were almost immediately erected, but the town was slow to grow into a metropolis. Perhaps because of the county's agrarian focus—it was supported by its growth of tobacco, wheat, Indian corn, barley, and oats—in its early years the town consisted only of the courthouse, one tavern, and about a dozen houses.

In the aftermath of the Revolutionary War, Charlottesville grew rapidly, in part because it was on the main state road to the West and was a logical stopping place for stagecoaches and travelers. In the early 1800s, the presence of Thomas Jefferson, James Monroe, and James Madison made it a center of social and political activity. The politicians' estates, Monticello, Ash Lawn, and Montpelier, bustled with high society and hosted national and foreign diplomats, including the Marquis de Lafayette. Good food and drink were of paramount importance at these plantations, and other area estates followed their lead. As the knowledge and skills Jefferson brought from Europe began to spread, Charlottesville became a center of culinary expertise.

Fresh garden produce, good and tender meat, fresh fish, and plenty of herbs and spices were as important to Charlottesville's early citizens as they are to residents today. In Richmond, tobacco, wheat, wool, and yarn were exchanged for sugar, spices, tea, and coffee. After the Civil War, from which the town emerged largely unscathed, Northern influences brought a diversification in local crops. Fruit crops took on increased importance, and apple orchards, peach orchards, and vineyards proliferated. Years after Jefferson had established his own vineyard with grapes brought from Paris, Albemarle County–grown wines began to win awards at international fairs and exhibitions.

Today, the beautiful grounds and neoclassical buildings of "Mr. Jefferson's University," the University of Virginia, are the cornerstone of a thriving, pleasant town with enviable surroundings: the gorgeous, gently rolling countryside of the Piedmont Plateau and the Blue Ridge mountains. The area is noted for its cultivation of grapes, peaches, and apples, as well as for its breeding of fine horses, sheep, and beef cattle.

# INTRODUCTION

Some basic information will enhance your enjoyment of this book and the dishes that result from its recipes.

**Microwave ovens**. Microwave ovens vary greatly in their wattage; that is, the power at which they cook. Cooking times given for recipes that involve microwaving must necessarily be vague. The recipes in this book were tested on a seven-hundred-watt oven, so these times may be longer than needed. It doesn't take long to become accustomed to the power of your microwave, and you'll be able to adjust the times given accordingly.

Don't forget that your microwave has settings other than high. Medium, or fifty percent power, melts butter quickly, warms breads without making them tough, and is generally as useful as high. This is especially true for microwave ovens with powers of one thousand watts or more.

**Butter and margarine**. The recipes in this book call for butter, but solid margarine may be substituted in most without a problem. Whipped and light butters and margarines, however, will not yield the same cooked dishes.

Many gourmet recipes call for unsalted butter and add salt later, as an ingredient. Because the average household does not stock both salted and unsalted butter, and because I've found the difference rarely noticeable, all but a few of these recipes call for salted butter and little or no additional salt.

**Herbs and spices**. Herbs and spices are meant to enhance flavors, not mask them, so use them sparingly. In most cases, don't add such seasonings until the main ingredients have been partially cooked.

When you substitute dried herbs for fresh, remember to use only one third as much. Dried herbs and spices are affected by age and heat, so throw away any that you've had for ten years. If in doubt, crush some in your hand and smell to see if it's still pungent.

Fresh herbs freeze well, so wash, pat dry, and freeze extras in a plastic bag. Parsley and chives, for example, are much better frozen than dried.

1

**Marinades.** Because acids tenderize meat, acidic ingredients like lemon juice, vinegar, and wine are important components of marinades. Do not marinate food in aluminum or tin pans; they react with this acidity. Use a glass, ceramic, or stainless-steel container, and cover and refrigerate marinating foods.

# BEVERAGES

Minted Iced Tea

Pink Lemonade

Tangy Tomato Juice

Cranberry Sangría

Fruit-Yogurt Shakes

Hot Mulled Cider

Real Hot Cocoa

Irish Coffee

Mexican Coffee

Sangría

Party Wine Punch

Tidewater Punch

Champagne Punch

Mixed Fruit Punch

## Minted Iced Tea

| | |
|---|---|
| 1 | cup sugar |
| ½ | cup water |
| 2 | tablespoons orange zest |
| ½ | cup fresh mint leaves, packed |
| 4 | cups strong tea |
| 1 | cup fresh orange juice |
| 2 | teaspoons fresh lemon juice |

1. In a small saucepan, simmer sugar, water, and orange zest for 5 minutes. Stir in mint leaves and remove from heat. Let sit for 5 minutes.
2. Fill a pitcher with tea, orange juice, and lemon juice. Stir.
3. Strain sugar mixture into pitcher. Chill. Serve with mint leaves if desired.

# Pink Lemonade

| 1 | cup water |
|---|---|
| 3/4 | cup sugar |
| 3 | cups cold water |
| 1 | cup fresh lemon juice |
| 1/2 | cup cranberry juice |

1. In a 2-cup measuring cup, heat 1 cup water and sugar in the microwave at high for about 2 minutes. Stir until sugar is dissolved.
2. Mix all ingredients. Pour over ice cubes or a ring of ice. Garnish with lemon slices, fresh mint leaves, and/or maraschino cherries if desired.

# Tangy Tomato Juice

| 1 | quart tomato juice |
|---|---|
| 1 | tablespoon Worcestershire sauce |
| 1/2 | teaspoon hot sauce |
| 1/2 | teaspoon dill weed |
| 1/2 | teaspoon ground celery seed |

1. Combine all ingredients and chill.

**Note**
Tangy Tomato Juice is a good base for a Bloody Mary as well as tasty by itself.

# Cranberry Sangría                              chill 3 hours

| 48 | ounces cranberry juice |
|---|---|
| 3 | cups port wine |
| | lemon slices for garnish |
| | orange slices for garnish |

1. Combine cranberry juice and wine.
2. Chill at least 3 hours.
3. Decorate with lemon and orange slices.

# Fruit-Yogurt Shakes

Delicious and nutritious drinks can be made from this recipe. The most popular is banana, but strawberry, peach, and raspberry fruit-yogurt shakes are excellent, too.

|       |                          |
|-------|--------------------------|
| 1/2   | cup vanilla yogurt       |
| 1/2   | cup milk                 |
| 1/2   | cup sliced fruit         |
| 1–3   | teaspoons sugar (see note) |
|       | ice cubes                |

1. Combine yogurt, milk, fruit, and sugar to taste.
2. Add two ice cubes and blend in a blender for approximately 1 minute.

**Note**
The optimal amount of sugar will vary with the tartness of the fruit.

# Hot Mulled Cider

|       |                            |
|-------|----------------------------|
| 4     | cups apple cider           |
| 2     | tablespoons dark brown sugar |
| 1     | stick (3 inches) cinnamon  |
| 1/2   | teaspoon allspice          |
| 1/2   | teaspoon whole cloves      |
|       | orange slices for garnish  |

1. In a saucepan, combine all ingredients and simmer for 10 to15 minutes.
2. Strain cider mixture through several layers of cheesecloth or a fine sieve.
3. Serve hot in mugs decorated with orange slices.

**Variation**
Add 1/4 cup brandy if desired.

# Real Hot Cocoa

On a damp and cold winter day, there's nothing better than a good cup of hot cocoa. So often we settle for a packet of cocoa and water, but the real thing is soooo good!

| | |
|---|---|
| 1 | tablespoon unsweetened cocoa (see note) |
| 1 | teaspoon sugar |
| 3/4 | cup milk (2% or richer) |
| 1/8 | teaspoon vanilla |
| | whipped cream or marshmallows |

1. In a saucepan, combine cocoa and sugar. Slowly add milk, whisking continuously.
2. Place over medium heat and stir well until bubbles appear at the sides of the pan. Remove from heat and stir in vanilla.
3. Top with whipped cream or marshmallows.

**Notes**

A quality Dutch process cocoa is preferred. It is less acidic and has better flavor.

To prevent a skin from forming on top of the cocoa, whisk briskly as soon as bubbles appear. That way, a foam will form on top.

# Irish Coffee

| | |
|---|---|
| 6 | ounces hot strong coffee |
| 1 | teaspoon sugar |
| 1 1/2 | ounces Irish whiskey |
| | whipped cream |

1. In a warm mug, combine coffee and sugar. Stir until sugar dissolves. Add whiskey.
2. Top with a dollop of whipped cream.

# Mexican Coffee

| | |
|---|---|
| 6 | ounces espresso or other strong coffee |
| 1/4 | cup heavy cream |
| 2 | teaspoons chocolate syrup |
| 1 | ounce Kahlúa |
| | whipped cream |

1. In a coffee mug, combine coffee, cream, and chocolate syrup. Microwave for about 2 minutes at medium-high.
2. Add Kahlúa and stir. Top with whipped cream if desired.


# Sangría

| | |
|---|---|
| 1 | orange |
| 1 | lemon |
| 1/4 | cup sugar |
| 1/4 | cup water |
| 3/4 | liter (1 bottle) dry red wine, chilled |
| 8 | ounces club soda, chilled |
| 2 | ounces brandy or Cognac |

1. Slice orange and lemon. Simmer half the slices in a saucepan with the sugar and water for about 3 minutes, until the sugar is dissolved. Let cool.
2. In a pitcher, combine wine, soda, reserved slices of fruit, brandy or Cognac, and sugar mixture (with or without simmered fruit).
3. Serve over ice.

# Party Wine Punch

1½     **liters (2 bottles) dry white wine, chilled**
4     **cups apple juice, chilled**
12     **ounces apricot nectar, chilled**

1.  Combine all ingredients in a punch bowl filled with a ring or block of ice.

**Yield: 20 servings**

# Tidewater Punch

³/₄     **liter bourbon, chilled**
12     **ounces frozen pineapple–orange juice concentrate, thawed**
³/₄     **cup lemon juice**
2     **liters lemon-lime carbonated drink, chilled**

1.  Combine bourbon and juices in a punch bowl.
2.  Add carbonated drink and serve.

# Champagne Punch

1½     **liters (2 bottles) sauterne, chilled**
½     **liter (1 bottle) dry Champagne, chilled**
1     **quart ginger ale, chilled**
      **fruit for garnish**

1.  Pour sauterne, Champagne, and ginger ale over an ice ring or block of ice in a punch bowl.
2.  Decorate with fruit slices.

# Mixed Fruit Punch

| | |
|---|---|
| 1½ | quarts canned pineapple juice |
| 1 | cup fresh orange juice |
| ½ | cup fresh lemon juice |
| 2 | tablespoons fresh lime juice |
| 1 | cup sugar |
| 2 | liters ginger ale, chilled |
| 1 | liter club soda, chilled |
| 1 | cup fresh strawberries, sliced |
| 1 | lemon, thinly sliced |
| 1 | orange, thinly sliced |

1. Combine juices with sugar and stir until sugar dissolves. Refrigerate at least 4 hours.
2. Stir in remaining ingredients.

**Yield: 20 servings**

### Variations

When strawberries are unavailable, use cubes of pineapple, mint leaves, or maraschino cherries.

Omit the club soda and add 5 cups of light rum or 2 bottles of white wine.

Meriwether Lewis, whose famous trek with William Clark opened the uncharted West, was born on August 18, 1774, at Locust Hill near Ivy Depot, just west of Charlottesville. His mother, Lucy Meriwether Lewis, was known for her splendid garden, and she ministered to the poor and ill with its herbs.

# APPETIZERS

# About Appetizers

Appetizers can also be side dishes, main meals, and snacks. The casual eating most of us do today requires a flexibility in food choices that makes it difficult to classify some dishes. Many times, an appetizer eaten over the sink has been my only sustenance on the way to a meeting, ball game, or similar commitment.

Most of these appetizers are just as good (and less caloric) with Neufchâtel cheese in place of cream cheese. I have not found a fat-free cheese that does as well. Serving baked chips or low-fat crackers is another way to make appetizers more healthful without sacrificing taste. Fresh fruits and vegetables, of course, make for the most nutritious starters.

## Quick Fixes

*With crackers, party rounds, or tortilla pieces, serve:*

1. Peanut butter with a dollop of horseradish in the center
2. Cream cheese with sliced black olives
3. Cream cheese with a dollop of Jezebel Sauce (page 21) on top
4. Salmon or shrimp paste
5. Cream cheese with a dollop of hot pepper jelly
6. Slices of Camembert, Havarti, or other cheeses
7. Blend of 1/2 avocado and 1/2 cup Stilton cheese
8. Cream cheese and chutney

*With fresh vegetables like carrot sticks, broccoli, cauliflower, cucumber sticks, celery, cherry tomatoes, and radishes, use the following combinations as a dip:*

1. Mustard and mayonnaise
2. Yogurt and salsa
3. Traditional French's onion dip in sour cream
4. 8 ounces cream cheese, 1 tablespoon horseradish, and 1/2 teaspoon hot sauce microwaved at medium for about 1 minute and stirred well
5. 1/2 cup mayonnaise and 1/2 teaspoon curry powder

*Fruit is quick and easy, too. Try:*

1. Apple and pear wedges tossed with a few drops of lemon juice (to prevent browning)
2. Fresh or canned pineapple chunks
3. Banana pieces, about 3/4-inch long, rolled in chopped peanuts
4. Seedless grapes or cherries
5. Peeled apple wedges rolled in cinnamon and sugar (a children's favorite)

## Note

Be sure to serve toothpicks alongside juicy fruit pieces for easy eating.

# The Original Swiss Cheese Fondue

**Schnitzelhouse Restaurant**
*Ed Gisler, Certified Executive Chef*

The secret to fondue is the right cheese, the right wine, the right equipment, and the right guests.

| | |
|---|---|
| 1 | clove garlic, peeled |
| 2 | cups dry white wine |
| ½ | pound Gruyère, grated |
| ½ | pound imported Swiss cheese, grated |
| 1 | teaspoon cornstarch |
| | freshly ground black pepper to taste |
| | freshly ground nutmeg to taste |
| | kirschwasser (optional) |
| 1 | loaf French bread or pain au levain, cut into cubes |

1. Rub Caquelon casserole (fondue pot) with garlic and then chop it. Pour wine into the pot, add garlic, and heat.
2. Combine cheeses and add cornstarch. Stirring constantly with a wooden spoon, add cheese mixture to the heating wine. Heat until all the cheese is melted, 10 to 12 minutes.
3. Season to taste with pepper, nutmeg, and kirschwasser, if desired.
4. Serve fondue on the special pot holder with alcohol burner and the bread in the bread basket. The fondue should continue to simmer very gently while guests help themselves with fondue forks.

## Variations
Different cheese combinations can be used. Stick with quality cheese for a quality fondue.

**Yield: 4 servings**

# Vietnamese Shrimp and Crab Fritters with Spicy Dipping Sauce

**Hamiltons' at First & Main**
*Bill Hamilton, Certified Executive Chef*

Sauce:

| | |
|---|---|
| 2 | teaspoons Vietnamese chili-garlic paste |
| | juice of 2 limes |
| 2 | tablespoons fish sauce |
| 1/4 | cup grated carrot |
| 1 | tablespoon sugar |
| 1/2 | cup water |

Fritters:

| | |
|---|---|
| 8 | ounces mild, light fish (e.g., sea bass, halibut, or grouper), cut into 1/2-inch cubes |
| 1 | egg white |
| 1 | tablespoon cornstarch |
| 1 | teaspoon Vietnamese chili-garlic paste (e.g., Rooster brand) |
| 1 | teaspoon minced fresh ginger |
| 1/2 | teaspoon minced fresh garlic |
| | juice of 2 limes |
| 1 | tablespoon fish sauce (nam pla) |
| 1/2 | teaspoon dark sesame oil |
| 1 | teaspoon sugar |
| 8 | ounces lump crabmeat, picked over |
| 8 | ounces cooked shrimp, chopped |
| 2 | tablespoons minced fresh cilantro |
| 1/4 | cup finely chopped sweet red pepper |
| | canola oil for frying |
| | Bibb lettuce leaves for garnish |
| | fresh cilantro sprigs for garnish |
| | lime wedges for garnish |

1. In a bowl, mix sauce ingredients well. Set aside.
2. Place fish, egg, cornstarch, chili-garlic paste, ginger, garlic, lime juice, fish sauce, sesame oil, and sugar in a food processor and puree until homogeneous but not quite smooth.
3. In a bowl, mix crabmeat, shrimp, cilantro, and red pepper by hand. Combine with processed ingredients.
4. Heat ½ inch oil in a heavy skillet until hot (350 degrees). Carefully drop rounded spoonfuls of fritter mixture into oil and fry in batches for 3 to 4 minutes, turning once, until cooked through.
5. Serve with Bibb lettuce leaves, fresh cilantro sprigs, lime wedges, and spicy dipping sauce.

**Yield: 8 servings**

# Tomato-Basil Tartlet

**High Meadows Inn**
*David J. Barbieri, Chef*

This recipe is much easier than it seems. After a little practice, you should be able to prepare half a dozen or a dozen tartlets in under an hour. They make a great appetizer or light lunch.

| | |
|---|---|
| 8 | ounces mozzarella, shredded |
| 4 | ounces chèvre (goat cheese) |
| 1 | cup grated Parmesan |
| | salt and pepper to taste |
| 1 | sheet puff pastry |
| 18 | leaves fresh basil |
| 6–8 | Roma tomatoes, sliced into thin circles |
| 2 | tablespoons extra virgin olive oil |
| 1 | teaspoon herbes de Provence or oregano |

1. Preheat oven to 375 degrees.
2. Combine mozzarella, chèvre, Parmesan, salt, and pepper and mix well.
3. Spray six 4-inch, fluted tartlet pans liberally with vegetable oil spray. Align pans and drape puff pastry over. Using a rolling pin, cut pastry to size. Gently remove excess dough and shape pastry to tartlet pans with your fingers.
4. Spread an equal amount of cheese mixture into each cup. Top with one or two fresh basil leaves. Decoratively arrange tomato slices on top of basil leaves. Drizzle olive oil over tomatoes and sprinkle with salt and herbes de Provence.
5. Bake at 375 degrees for 25 to 30 minutes, until pastry is golden brown, tomatoes appear cooked, and cheese is hot. Let cool slightly.
6. Pile remaining basil leaves on top of one another, forming a small bunch. Gently fold leaves over themselves. Using a sharp chef's knife, cut basil crosswise into thin strips.
7. Turn tartlets out of pans. Serve warm on plates decorated with a sprinkle of basil chiffonade.

**Yield: 6 servings**

# Garlic-Encrusted Tuna with Ginger Sauce on Wilted Watercress

**Caffe Bocce**
*Marcia I. Miller, Chef/Co-Owner*

| | |
|---|---|
| 1 | egg |
| 1 | teaspoon chopped ginger |
| 1/2 | cup bread crumbs |
| 1 1/2 | teaspoons minced garlic |
| 6 | ounces sushi-quality tuna |
| | salt and pepper to taste |
| | flour for dredging |
| 1/2 | teaspoon butter |
| 2 | teaspoons olive oil |
| 1/4 | cup white wine |
| 1 | teaspoon chopped shallots |
| 1/4 | cup cream |
| 1 | bunch watercress |

1. In a bowl, combine egg and ginger and mix well.
2. Combine bread crumbs and 1 teaspoon of the garlic on a flat plate or clean surface.
3. Season tuna with salt and pepper and coat with flour. Slap to remove excess flour.
4. Dip tuna in egg mixture and then roll in the bread crumb mixture.
5. In a hot pan, heat butter and 1 teaspoon of the olive oil. Sear tuna on both sides (1 to 2 minutes for rare). Remove tuna and let rest.
6. Deglaze pan with white wine. Add shallots and remaining garlic and cook until reduced by half. Add cream and whisk in remaining egg mixture. Continue to whisk until sauce thickens. Add salt and pepper to taste.
7. In a small pan, slightly wilt watercress in remaining olive oil. Mound on a plate.
8. Slice tuna on the bias and arrange atop watercress. Lace with sauce and serve.

# Hot Crab Dip

| | |
|---|---|
| 16 | ounces cream cheese, softened |
| 1 | cup shredded cheddar cheese |
| 1 | cup light sour cream |
| 1/2 | tablespoon lemon juice |
| 4 | teaspoons mayonnaise |
| 1 | pound crabmeat, picked of cartilage and shell |
| 2 | teaspoons Worcestershire sauce |
| 1 | teaspoon mustard |
| 1/4 | teaspoon garlic salt |

1. Preheat oven to 350 degrees.
2. Cream cheeses and mix in sour cream, lemon juice, and mayonnaise.
3. Mix in remaining ingredients.
4. Bake for 30 to 40 minutes.

# Hot Asparagus Dip

| | |
|---|---|
| 1 | can (15 ounces) asparagus, drained |
| 1/4 | cup Hellmann's mayonnaise |
| 1/2 | cup plain yogurt |
| 1/2 | cup grated Parmesan |
| 1/4 | teaspoon minced garlic |
| 1/2 | teaspoon freshly ground black pepper |

1. Preheat oven to 350 degrees.
2. Cut asparagus into 1-inch pieces and combine with other ingredients.
3. Bake in an 8 x 8-inch pan until dip bubbles, about 15 minutes.
4. Serve with crackers.

# Hot Artichoke Dip

| | |
|---|---|
| 1 | can (15 ounces) artichoke hearts, drained and cut in pieces |
| 8 | ounces cream cheese, softened |
| 1/2 | cup mayonnaise |
| 4 | ounces mozzarella, shredded |
| 1 | cup grated Parmesan |
| 1/8 | teaspoon garlic powder |

1. Preheat oven to 350 degrees.
2. In a bowl, mix all ingredients until well blended. Transfer to a casserole dish.
3. Bake for 10 minutes. Stir and return to oven for another 5 minutes. Should be hot and bubbly.

# Swiss Cheese and Almond Spread

| | |
|---|---|
| 1/3 | cup sliced almonds |
| 8 | ounces cream cheese, softened |
| 1 1/2 | cups shredded Swiss cheese |
| 1/2 | cup Miracle Whip |
| 2 | tablespoons chopped green onion |

1. Preheat oven to 350 degrees.
2. In the oven, toast almonds for 5 minutes.
3. Combine all ingredients in a bowl and mix well.
4. Spread mixture in a 9-inch pie pan and bake for 12 minutes.
5. Serve with crackers.

# Yogurt Dip

| | |
|---|---|
| 6 | ounces vanilla yogurt |
| 2 | tablespoons maple syrup |
| 1/2 | teaspoon lemon juice |

1. Combine all ingredients.
2. Serve cold with assorted fruit.

# Party Spinach Dip

8   ounces cream cheese or Neufchâtel

10  ounces frozen chopped spinach, thawed

2   cups shredded Cheddar

1/2 cup chopped onion

1   cup diced tomato

1. Microwave cream cheese at medium for 1 minute to soften.
2. Squeeze spinach to remove as much liquid as possible.
3. Combine all ingredients in a microwavable bowl.
4. Microwave at medium for 6 to 10 minutes, stirring several times, until cheese is melted.
5. Serve with crackers or chunks of bread (see note).

## Note
Party Spinach Dip is often served in a round, hollowed-out loaf of pumpernickel or sourdough bread. Bread from the middle of the loaf is used for dipping.

# Onion Rounds

1/3 cup mayonnaise

1/3 cup grated Parmesan

20  party rye or baguette slices

20  thin slices of onion

1. Mix mayonnaise and cheese. Spread on rounds of bread.
2. Place rounds on a cookie sheet, top with onion slices, and broil about 5 inches from heat for 3 to 5 minutes, until brown and bubbly.

# Spinach-Cheese Squares

| | |
|---|---|
| 1 | cup flour |
| 1 | teaspoon salt |
| 1 | teaspoon baking powder |
| 1 | cup milk |
| 1/4 | cup butter, melted |
| 3 | eggs, beaten |
| 1 | pound Monterey Jack, grated |
| 4 | cups chopped fresh spinach |
| 1/4 | teaspoon nutmeg |

1. Preheat oven to 375 degrees.
2. In a mixing bowl, blend flour, salt, and baking powder. Beat in milk, butter, and eggs. Fold in cheese and spinach.
3. Place in a 9 x 13-inch pan and sprinkle with nutmeg. Bake for 35 to 40 minutes. Let cool 10 minutes before cutting.

**Yield: 32 2-inch squares**


# Tasty Southern Pecans

| | |
|---|---|
| 3 | cups pecan halves |
| 1/4 | cup melted butter |
| 1 1/2 | teaspoons ground cumin |
| 1/4 | teaspoon cayenne |
| 2 | tablespoons sugar |
| 1/2 | teaspoon salt |

1. Preheat oven to 300 degrees.
2. Combine all ingredients and mix well.
3. Spread coated pecans in a single layer on a cookie sheet.
4. Bake for 20 minutes, stirring once.

# Spinach Balls

| | |
|---|---|
| 1 | package (10 ounces) frozen chopped spinach |
| 3 | eggs |
| 1/2 | cup finely chopped onion |
| 2/3 | cup grated Parmesan |
| 1/4 | teaspoon ground pepper |
| 8 | ounces herbed bread stuffing |
| 2 | tablespoons melted butter |

1. Preheat oven to 350 degrees.
2. Squeeze spinach between paper towels to remove as much water as possible.
3. In a mixing bowl, beat eggs well and add onion, cheese, and pepper. Add spinach, stuffing, and butter and allow moisture to soften stuffing.
4. Shape into balls about 1 inch in diameter and place on a greased cookie sheet.
5. Bake balls for about 10 minutes.

**Note**
These can be frozen before or after baking and are an excellent choice for the busy cook.

# Jezebel Sauce

| | |
|---|---|
| 1 | jar (16 ounces) apricot preserves |
| 1 | jar (16 ounces) pineapple preserves |
| 2 | ounces Coleman's mustard |
| 6 | ounces coarse hot horseradish |
| 2 | teaspoons cracked black pepper |

1. Mix all ingredients and chill.
2. Serve with crackers and cream cheese or as a condiment with ham.

**Note**
Jezebel Sauce will keep for a year in the fridge and makes a great gift.

# Guacamole

Guacamole is an excellent accompaniment to Mexican entrées and tortilla chips.

- 1/2    teaspoon minced garlic
- 1/2    cup sliced onion
- 1/4    cup fresh lemon juice
- 1      tablespoon olive oil
- 1/4    cup peeled diced tomatoes
- 2      ripe avocados
- 1/8    teaspoon Tabasco or other hot sauce

1. In a food processor, blend garlic, onion, lemon juice, and oil well.
2. Add tomato to mixture in processor and pulse until slightly chunky.
3. Halve, pit, and peel avocados. Add to mixture in food processor and pulse.
4. Add Tabasco and stir well.

**Note**

These measurements can be varied according to taste.

**Variation**

Substitute lime juice for lemon juice.

# Low-Calorie Guacamole                                chill 1 hour

- 1      large ripe avocado
- 1      medium ripe tomato, seeded and diced
- 1/3    cup finely diced onion
- 1/3    cup reduced-fat ricotta
- 2      tablespoons fresh lime juice
- 2      fresh jalapeños, seeded and minced
- 1/2    teaspoon salt

1. Mash avocado, tomato, onion, and cheese together until well blended.
2. Season with lime juice, peppers, and salt. Refrigerate for at least 1 hour to blend flavors.
3. Serve with baked tostados for a low-calorie appetizer.

# Curry Dip

chill 2 hours

- 1   cup mayonnaise
- 1   teaspoon horseradish
- 1   tablespoon curry powder
- 1   teaspoon grated onion
- 1   teaspoon lemon juice

1. Combine all ingredients.
2. Refrigerate for at least 2 hours before serving with vegetables or chunks of pita.


# Orange Marshmallow Dip

chill 2 to 3 hours

- 2   eggs, beaten
- 1/2   cup orange juice
- 1/4   cup sugar
- 2   teaspoons grated orange peel
- 2   cups miniature marshmallows

1. Combine eggs, orange juice, and sugar in a microwavable bowl.
2. Microwave at medium for 5 to 7 minutes, stirring occasionally, until thickened.
3. Add orange peel and marshmallows and microwave another 2 minutes. Stir until marshmallows are melted.
4. Refrigerate overnight or for several hours before serving with fruit.

# Taco Pie

2    large flour tortillas

8    ounces cream cheese, softened

8    ounces sour cream

1    cup finely chopped lettuce

1    cup finely chopped tomato

8    ounces Cheddar, shredded

1    cup salsa

1    green pepper, chopped

1    cup chopped ripe olives

1. Spray tortillas with olive oil and bake at 350 degrees for 5 minutes.
2. Combine cream cheese and sour cream and set aside.
3. On each tortilla, layer lettuce, tomatoes, cheese, and salsa in that order. Top with sour cream mixture.
4. Sprinkle with pepper and olives, cut into wedges, and serve.

**Variation**

Spread lettuce, tomato, cheese, and salsa on a serving plate and top with sour cream mixture, pepper, and olives. Serve as a dip with tortilla chips.

# Hot Swiss and Turkey Rounds

| | |
|---|---|
| 1 | teaspoon chicken bouillon |
| 1 | cup milk |
| 3 | tablespoons butter |
| 2 | tablespoons flour |
| 1 | cup shredded Swiss cheese |
| 20 | party rye or baguette slices |
| 6 | ounces deli turkey, thinly sliced |
| 1/2 | cup thinly sliced onion |
| 5 | strips of bacon, cooked and crumbled |
| | parsley for garnish |

1. Preheat oven to 350 degrees.
2. In the microwave, at high for 1 minute, dissolve bouillon in milk.
3. In a saucepan, melt butter. Stir in flour. Over medium heat, whisk in milk mixture and cook, whisking continuously, until sauce thickens to a smooth roux. Stir in Swiss cheese and continue to whisk until smooth.
4. Place rounds of bread on a baking tray and top each with a bit of turkey and onion, a tablespoon of sauce, and a bit of bacon.
5. Bake for 10 minutes.
6. Garnish with parsley and serve.

# Crispy Tostados

These can be used as a base for many appetizers. Top them with cheese and salsa, avocado, refried beans, feta cheese and ripe olives, thin slices of sweet onion, diced tomato, and shredded lettuce. The list is endless.

| | |
|---|---|
| 4 | flour tortillas |
| 1 1/2 | teaspoons olive oil |

1. Preheat oven to 375 degrees.
2. Brush or spray tortillas on both sides with oil.
3. Bake for 6 to 8 minutes, until crisp and golden.

# Vidalia Onion

1     large Vidalia onion
1     beef bouillon cube
1     slice mozzarella

1. Peel onion and slice bottom so it will stand.
2. Cut a cone one inch deep in the top of the onion. Reserve cutaway portion.
3. Set bouillon cube in cavity and place reserved cone on top of the onion.
4. Microwave until soft, at high for 3 to 5 minutes. Place cheese on top and microwave until just melted, another 30 seconds.
5. Slice before serving.

# Cheese Pastries

These pastries are a treat with virtually any filling. The possibilities include dates cooked with brown sugar and a little cinnamon; tuna fish with finely chopped pickle and a little mayonnaise; and crabmeat with a blend of celery, white wine, mustard, and mayonnaise. Filled with seasoned chopped meat or fish, Cheese Pastries can also serve as an entrée.

$1/2$     cup cold butter
$1^1/2$     cups flour
$1/2$     teaspoon salt
2     cups grated sharp cheese
$1/8$     teaspoon cayenne (optional)
    filling of your choice

1. Preheat oven to 350 degrees.
2. With a pastry cutter or fork, cut butter into flour and salt.
3. Mix in cheese and optional cayenne. Form mixture into a ball, adding a few drops of water if necessary.
4. Roll out pastry and cut according to use. To make small tarts, cut into rounds or 2 x 3-inch rectangles.
5. Place a teaspoon of filling to one side. Fold over and pinch edges.
6. Bake about 12 minutes, until slightly browned.

# Shrimp Toast Rounds

| | |
|---|---|
| 1/4 | cup water |
| 1 | tablespoon cornstarch |
| 1/4 | cup flour |
| 1/2 | teaspoon sesame oil |
| 1/4 | teaspoon sugar |
| 1/2 | teaspoon salt |
| 1/4 | teaspoon ground pepper |
| 1 | large egg, slightly whisked |
| 1/2 | pound uncooked shrimp, peeled and deveined |
| 1/2 | cup chopped green onion |
| 20 | party rye or baguette slices |

1. Preheat oven to 450 degrees. Spray a cookie sheet with oil.
2. In a medium bowl, combine water and cornstarch. Add flour and sesame oil, sugar, salt, and pepper. Stir in egg.
3. Cut shrimp into 1/2-inch pieces. Add shrimp and onion to bowl and mix well.
4. Spread a tablespoon of the shrimp mixture on each round and place on cookie sheet. Spray the entire collection with oil.
5. Bake for about 15 minutes, until the edges of the bread are golden brown.


# Tortilla Rollups                                chill 2 to 3 hours

| | |
|---|---|
| 8 | ounces cream cheese, softened |
| 4 | ounces fresh or canned green chili peppers, chopped fine |
| 3 | green onions, chopped fine |
| 1/4 | teaspoon garlic powder |
| 3–4 | large flour tortillas |
| | salsa |

1. Mix cream cheese, peppers, onions, and garlic powder.
2. Spread cream cheese mixture on tortillas and roll up. Wrap in plastic film and refrigerate for several hours.
3. Slice into bite-size pieces and serve with a side of salsa.

# Marinated Broccoli

|   |   |
|---|---|
| 3 | cups broccoli flowerets |
| 1/2 | cup white wine vinegar |
| 1/4 | cup canola oil |
| 2 | teaspoons sugar |
| 2 | teaspoons dill weed |
| 1/4 | teaspoon ground pepper |
| 1/4 | teaspoon garlic salt |

1. Combine all ingredients and mix well.
2. Marinate flowerets in the refrigerator for 24 hours, turning about every 6 hours.
3. Drain. Serve broccoli chilled and with toothpicks.

## Variations

This recipe could include cauliflowerets, mushroom caps, and large pitted black olives.

For more zip, substitute oregano for the dill and add Tabasco.

# Water Chestnuts with Bacon

|   |   |
|---|---|
| 8 | ounces whole water chestnuts |
| 2 | tablespoons maple syrup |
| 1 | pound bacon |

1. Cut water chestnuts in half and dip in maple syrup. Cut bacon strips in half.
2. Wrap bacon strips around water chestnuts and secure with toothpicks.
3. On a microwavable bacon grill or plate lined with paper towels, microwave at high for 4 minutes. Turn and microwave another 4 minutes, until crisp.

## Variation

Bake at 450 degrees for 20 minutes, then broil (turning regularly) until done.

# Banana-Peanut Rolls

| | |
|---|---|
| 2 | burrito-size flour tortillas |
| 2 | ripe bananas |
| 2 | tablespoons raisins |
| 2 | tablespoons fresh lime juice |
| 1 | teaspoon grated ginger |
| 1/2 | small jalapeño, diced fine |
| 1/2 | teaspoon allspice |
| 1/2 | cup creamy peanut butter |
| 1/4 | cup honey-roasted peanuts |
| 4 | lettuce leaves |

1. Heat tortillas in the microwave at high for 30 seconds.
2. Dice bananas and mix with raisins, lime juice, ginger, jalapeño, and allspice.
3. Spread half the peanut butter on each tortilla. Spread half the banana mixture on top of the peanut butter on each tortilla.
4. Sprinkle with peanuts and put 2 lettuce leaves on each.
5. Roll up and slice tortillas into 1 1/2-inch pieces.
6. Wrap in plastic film and refrigerate for an hour or two.

## Note

Banana-Peanut Rolls make great sandwiches, too. Just cut each tortilla in half.

# Parmesan Pastry Sticks

| | |
|---|---|
| ¼ | cup grated Parmesan |
| 1 | tablespoon finely chopped fresh parsley |
| ½ | teaspoon crushed dried oregano |
| 1 | egg, beaten |
| 1 | tablespoon water |
| ½ | package (17 ounces) frozen puff pastry, thawed |

1. Preheat oven to 400 degrees.
2. Combine cheese, parsley, and oregano in a bowl. Mix egg and water in a cup.
3. On a lightly floured surface, unfold puff pastry and roll into 14 x 10-inch rectangle. Cut into two 5 x 14-inch pieces and brush both with the egg wash. Top one pastry piece with the cheese mixture and cover it with the other, egg-side down. Roll with a rolling pin to seal pieces together.
4. Cut into 5 x ½-inch strips. Place on a greased cookie sheet. Twist and press down the ends. Bake 10 minutes.

**Yield: 28 sticks**

---

*The mountains were grand, yesterday. Still are, since I can see the Blue Ridge from both my windows. I can see all Charlottesville, and the University, too. The fall coloring is splendid here—yellow hickory and red gum and sumach and laurel with the blue-green pines. It's just grand.*

—**William Faulkner**, in a 1931 letter to his wife, Estelle

# Cheese Crisps

chill 2 to 3 hours

| | |
|---|---|
| 1/2 | pound sharp Cheddar, grated |
| 1/2 | cup Parmesan, grated |
| 1/2 | cup butter |
| 1/4 | cup water |
| 3/4 | cup whole wheat flour |
| 1/2 | cup white flour |
| 1/4 | teaspoon salt |
| 1/8 | teaspoon cayenne |
| 1 | cup rolled oats |

1. Preheat oven to 400 degrees.
2. In a large bowl, blend cheeses, butter, and water.
3. Add flours, salt, and cayenne. Stir in oats.
4. Divide dough in half. Form into two rolls about 1 1/2 inches thick. Wrap tightly in plastic film.
5. Refrigerate for several hours, until well chilled.
6. Cut into slices 1/8- to 1/4-inch thick. On a greased baking sheet, bake for 8 to 10 minutes. Let cool on a rack.

**Yield: 4 dozen slices**

**Note**

Wrapped in plastic, unbaked Cheese Crisps will keep for a week in the refrigerator.

# Pickled Shrimp

marinate 4 to 6 hours

| | |
|---|---|
| 1 | pound shrimp, cooked and cleaned |
| 4 | teaspoons lemon juice |
| 2 | cups thinly sliced onion |
| 1/2 | cup thinly sliced celery |
| 1/2 | teaspoon crushed garlic |
| 1 | cup vinegar |
| 1/2 | cup catsup |
| 1/2 | cup chili sauce |
| 1 | teaspoon salt |
| 2 | teaspoons Worcestershire sauce |
| 1/4 | teaspoon Tabasco |
| 1/2 | teaspoon dry mustard |

1. Sprinkle shrimp with lemon juice and refrigerate in a covered bowl or plastic bag with onion and celery for several hours.
2. In a saucepan, combine remaining ingredients and boil for about 5 minutes. Pour over shrimp and chill for several more hours.
3. Drain and serve with toothpicks.

# Make-Ahead Mushroom Croustades

These pastries are a big success at parties and picnics. They are also a nice treat to have in the freezer when company drops by.

| | |
|---|---|
| 2 | tablespoons soft butter |
| 24 | very thin slices white bread |
| 4 | tablespoons butter |
| 3 | tablespoons finely chopped shallots |
| 1/2 | pound mushrooms, finely chopped |
| 2 | tablespoons flour |
| 1 | cup heavy cream |
| 1/2 | teaspoon salt |
| 1/8 | teaspoon cayenne |
| 1 | tablespoon finely chopped chives |
| 1/2 | teaspoon lemon juice |
| 2 | tablespoons grated Parmesan |

1. Preheat oven to 400 degrees.
2. Coat the inside of tiny muffin tins heavily with 2 tablespoons soft butter.
3. Cut a 3-inch round from each slice of bread and fit these carefully into the tins, molding the bread so that it lines the cups. Bake for 10 minutes, until lightly browned. Remove from oven but leave in muffin tins. Turn oven down to 375 degrees.
4. In a frying pan, melt 4 tablespoons butter until foamy. Add shallots. Cook, stirring, over moderate heat about 4 minutes. Do not brown.
5. Stir in mushrooms and mix well. Cook 10 to 15 minutes, stirring occasionally, until the moisture has evaporated.
6. Remove pan from heat, sprinkle flour over mushrooms, and stir well. Pour heavy cream over all and return pan to low heat. Stir until cream just starts to boil. Remove from heat and stir in salt, cayenne, chives, and lemon juice.
7. Mound filling in the tiny bread cups. Sprinkle with cheese and dot with more butter. Bake at 375 degrees about 15 minutes, until bubbly. Remove from oven and let cool. Serve or store in resealable plastic bags in the freezer.
8. Before serving, remove from bags and bake at 375 degrees for about 20 minutes, until bubbly.

# SOUPS

# About Soups

Soups are very versatile foods. They can accompany a meal or be a full meal. Bean soups, vegetable-meat soups, and split pea soups especially are full meals unto themselves.

Most soups are best the day after they are made, as the flavors blend, but they can be made in quantity and frozen in suitable portions. Stored this way, they keep for months. It is great to heat something in the microwave and have a good meal, perhaps with a baguette from the bakery or a French roll from the freezer.

In many of these recipes the amount of salt is not designated. Canned broths contain varying amounts of salt, which makes it difficult to determine a single appropriate amount. Do be careful when adding extra salt; too much will not enhance your soup.

Many people like their soups somewhat spicy. I have found that the easiest way to give soups zip is to add some chilies or chilies and tomatoes. I suggest the Rotel brand because it is readily available and does the job very easily. Those who like a milder soup should cut down on this ingredient or omit it.

You can also flavor soups with bay leaves, which especially enhance bean and vegetable soups. However, people do not digest them, and they have been blamed for intestinal lesions. Always remove bay leaves before serving. Except in a few recipes, I have not suggested their use.

Celery leaves also provide good flavor and should be included when cutting celery for soups. Don't hesitate to use green onion tops or outside (clean) cabbage leaves when making stock; these are flavorful and would otherwise be discarded. Strain them from stock before using.

Another thing to keep in mind is that cream soups made with milk rather than cream will curdle if boiled unless you first add cornstarch or flour. If your soup does curdle, the addition of a small amount of cream will improve it.

In warm weather, cold soups can be as refreshing as hot soups are comforting in winter. I have included recipes for several cold soups that are delicious and easy to make.

# Making a Roux

Ever made a cream soup and wanted to thicken it quickly?

Begin with equal amounts of butter and flour and 1 cup liquid (water, milk, or cream) for every 2 tablespoons butter.

In a 1-quart Pyrex measuring cup or bowl, microwave 2 tablespoons butter at high for 30 seconds. Whisk in 2 tablespoons flour. Microwave at high for 30 seconds and whisk well. Whisk in $1/2$ the liquid and microwave at high for 1 minute. Add the rest of the liquid and microwave for another $1^1/2$ minutes. Times are approximate.

# Fresh Pea and Sorrel Soup

**Clifton, The Country Inn**
*Rachel Greenberg, Executive Chef*

| | |
|---|---|
| 3 | leeks (white and light green parts), washed and sliced crosswise |
| 2 | medium onions |
| 3 | tablespoons butter |
| | salt and pepper |
| 4 | large Yukon Gold potatoes, peeled and diced |
| 6 | cups vegetable broth |
| 3 | cups shelled peas |
| 2 | cups packed chopped sorrel leaves |
| 1–1½ | cups cream |
| | sugar to taste |
| | mint or dill for garnish |

1. In a large saucepan, sauté leeks and onions in butter over medium heat until soft. Season with salt and pepper.
2. Add potatoes and broth and let simmer until potatoes are soft. Do not overcook.
3. Add peas and cook for 5 to 10 minutes.
4. Add sorrel and transfer all to blender. Puree. Add cream, salt, pepper, and sugar to taste.
5. Garnish with mint, dill, sour cream, or crème fraîche. Serve immediately; soup will darken with time.

# Lobster–Sweet Corn Chowder

**Boar's Head Inn**
*Ken Harnad, Director of Food and Beverage*

| | |
|---|---|
| 4 | 1¹/₂-pound live lobsters, preferably female |
| ¹/₄ | cup olive oil |
| 4 | ounces sweet sugar-cured bacon or pancetta, cut into ¹/₂-inch dice (approximately 1 cup) |
| 1 | cup leek rounds (white and light parts only), washed |
| 1 | cup peeled and diced onions |
| 1 | cup sliced celery |
| 1 | cup peeled and sliced carrots |
| 2 | sprigs fresh thyme |
| ¹/₄ | teaspoon cumin seeds |
| ¹/₄ | teaspoon coriander seeds |
| ¹/₂ | teaspoon cayenne |
| ¹/₄ | teaspoon black peppercorns |
| 2 | cups white wine |
| 2 | cups heavy cream |
| 6 | ears of corn, kernels removed and reserved and cobs cut into 1-inch pieces |
| 2 | cups water |
| 1 | teaspoon kosher salt |
| ¹/₈ | teaspoon freshly ground black pepper |
| 1¹/₂ | cups diced new potatoes |
| 1 | red pepper, seeded, roasted, and diced |
| 2 | teaspoons seeded and minced jalapeño |
| 2 | tablespoons chopped parsley or cilantro |

1. Place a lobster belly-side down on a cutting board and hold it firmly at its midsection. Place the point of a large kitchen knife about midway down the head, with the sharp edge facing toward the head. With one strong motion, pierce downward and slice forward with the knife, splitting the top portion of the lobster's head and killing it instantly. Set aside and repeat with remaining lobsters.

2. Separate the tails from the bodies and remove the claws. Cut each tail into 4 even pieces. Split the heads and remove the light green liver (tomalley)

and the dark green roe (from the female lobster). Set aside the tails, claws, and heads.

3.  Using a rubber spatula, pass the tomalley and roe through a strainer into a small bowl. Cover the bowl and refrigerate.

4.  Heat olive oil over moderate heat in a Dutch oven or soup pot. Add the pancetta or bacon and cook, stirring occasionally, until brown. Add leeks and cook until wilted, about 2 minutes. Remove leeks and pancetta and reserve.

5.  Raise the heat to high and add lobster tail pieces, claws, and heads. Cook, stirring frequently, for 5 to 7 minutes, until bright red. Remove lobsters from pot and set aside to cool.

6.  Add onions, celery, carrots, thyme, cumin, coriander, cayenne, and black peppercorns to the pot. Lower the heat to medium and cook 10 minutes, until the vegetables are soft but not brown. Remove pot from heat.

7.  Crack open lobster tails and claws and remove the meat. Return shells and heads to the pot. Cut meat and claws into bite-size pieces and reserve, covered.

8.  Pour white wine into the pot and cook over medium heat until reduced by half. Add cream, corncob pieces, and 2 cups water. Lower the heat and let simmer, covered, for 5 minutes. Strain in a colander, pressing the solids to extract the maximum amount of liquid. Season with salt and pepper. This liquid is the chowder base.

9.  Return chowder base to the pot and add potatoes, red pepper, jalapeño, corn kernels, and reserved leeks and pancetta. Simmer gently until the potatoes are cooked, 7 to 10 minutes. Add reserved lobster meat to the chowder.

10.  Ladle a small amount of hot chowder into the bowl with the tomalley-roe mixture to warm slightly. Slowly stir the warmed roe mixture back into the chowder.

11.  Heat over low heat, stirring, until the roe turns the chowder light pink. Do not boil or the roe will separate. Ladle into warm bowls, sprinkle with chopped parsley or cilantro, and serve.

**Yield: 4 to 6 servings**

# Champagne and Brie Onion Soup

**The Tea Room Cafe at Starr Hill**
*Vickie and Mark Gresge, Proprietors*

| | |
|---|---|
| 1 | cup chopped celery |
| 1 | cup chopped carrots |
| 2 | cloves garlic, minced |
| 3 | cups chopped onion |
| 1 | cup peeled, chopped Granny Smith apple |
| 1/2 | cup butter |
| 1/4 | teaspoon ground pepper |
| 1/2 | teaspoon nutmeg |
| 8 | cups beef stock |
| 2 1/2 | cups Brut Champagne |
| 1/4 | pound Brie, at room temperature |

1. In a heavy soup pot over medium heat, sauté celery, carrots, garlic, onion, and apple in butter until soft. Stir, cover, and let simmer for 10 minutes.
2. Remove cover and add pepper, nutmeg, and 3 cups of the stock. Cover and simmer for an additional 20 minutes.
3. Pour into blender and blend until smooth. Return to soup pot.
4. Add Champagne and remaining broth. Mix well and simmer another 5 minutes.
5. Trim the crust from the Brie. The cheese should be soft and runny. Stir into the hot soup and mix well with a whisk. Simmer for 20 minutes over very low heat. Add salt if desired.
6. Serve with warm French bread.

**Yield: 4 to 6 servings**

# Roasted Chestnut Soup with Apple Crème Fraîche (optional)

**Prospect Hill, The Virginia Plantation Inn**
*The Sheehan Family, Innkeepers*

| | |
|---|---|
| 1/2 | crisp, tart apple, pureed or finely chopped |
| | pinch cinnamon |
| 1 | cup crème fraîche, at room temperature |
| 1 | onion, chopped |
| 1 | teaspoon butter |
| 3/4 | cup dry vermouth |
| 2 | cups chicken stock |
| 2 | cups chestnuts, peeled and roasted slightly at 350 degrees |
| 1 | tablespoon chopped fresh parsley |
| 1 | cup milk |
| | cracked black pepper to taste |
| 1 | teaspoon freshly ground nutmeg |

1. Stir apple and cinnamon into crème fraîche. Let stand 1/2 hour.
2. Sauté onion in butter in a large saucepan over medium heat until translucent. Deglaze pan with vermouth and add stock.
3. Add chestnuts and parsley. Cook at a simmer until chestnuts are soft. Transfer all to a food processor and puree until smooth. Return to heat and add milk slowly while stirring. Add pepper and nutmeg to taste.
4. Garnish with apple crème fraîche and serve hot.

# Homemade Chicken Broth

Good-tasting, low-salt chicken broth is difficult to purchase. Commercial brands of broth are certainly handy, but 1 cup typically contains 1,000 mg of sodium, or forty-two percent of your daily allotment. Even the so-called healthful varieties have 500 mg of sodium. Flavorful chicken broth that's good for you almost has to be made at home, and doing so really isn't time consuming.

I purchase the cheapest chicken parts—except for wings, which are too fatty—and let them cook for a while in a pot of water with some celery and onion and a little garlic. Then I remove the chicken and set it aside to cool. Skim any excess fat (a little makes things taste better) off the broth. Use the broth immediately or freeze it for future use. Freeze the chicken in plastic bags and use the meat in soups, salads, stir-fries, or sandwiches. For those who need it, here's a recipe:

3   pounds chicken parts with bones and skin
2   quarts water
4   stalks celery with leaves, chopped
1   cup chopped onion
1   teaspoon minced garlic

1.  With a small knife, remove any excess fat from the chicken. Place water, chicken, celery, onion, and garlic in a large covered saucepan and boil gently for 30 minutes.
2.  Remove meat pieces from pot. Use in soups, salads, or casseroles.
3.  The remaining stock can be used as is, strained, refrigerated for up to 3 days, or frozen for up to 6 months. Skim off any fat that comes to the top.

# Homemade Chicken Noodle Soup

Great for colds or whatever ails you.

|     |                                          |
|-----|------------------------------------------|
| 1   | cup cooked diced chicken                 |
| 3   | cups homemade chicken broth (page 41)    |
| 1–2 | cups water                               |
| 1/2 | teaspoon salt                            |
| 1   | teaspoon parsley flakes                  |
| 1/4 | teaspoon oregano                         |
| 1/4 | teaspoon ground allspice                 |
| 2   | ounces dry noodles                       |

1. Bring chicken, broth, water, and seasonings to a boil.
2. Add noodles and cook until tender.

**Yield: 3 cups**


# Zucchini Soup

|     |                            |
|-----|----------------------------|
| 1   | pound zucchini, sliced     |
| 1/2 | cup chopped onion          |
| 2   | cups chicken broth         |
| 2   | tablespoons butter         |
| 1   | teaspoon salt              |
| 1   | teaspoon curry powder      |
|     | sour cream for garnish     |

1. In a saucepan over medium-high heat, cook zucchini and onion in 1 cup of the broth until tender. Add butter, salt, and curry.
2. Transfer to blender and add second cup of broth. Blend.
3. Serve hot or cold with a dollop of sour cream.

# White Fish Stock

| | |
|---|---|
| 1–2 | pounds bones, trimmings, or unseasoned leftovers of white fish, such as haddock, flounder, or whiting |
| 1 | cup sliced onion |
| 1/2 | cup chopped parsley and stems |
| 2 | teaspoons fresh lemon juice |
| 1/2 | teaspoon salt |
| 1/2 | cup celery pieces |
| 1/2 | teaspoon ground pepper |
| 1/2 | cup dry white wine (optional) |
| 31/2–5 | cups water |

1. In a large pot, combine fish, onion, parsley, lemon juice, and salt. Cover and steam slowly for about 5 minutes.
2. Add remaining ingredients and cook over medium heat for 25 minutes. Do not cook longer.
3. Skim off froth and strain through a fine sieve.
4. Freeze or use in fish soups and stew.

**Yield: 4 cups**

# New England Fish Chowder

| | |
|---|---|
| 3 | slices bacon |
| 2 | cups fish stock or chicken broth |
| 1 | cup thinly sliced onions |
| 1/4 | teaspoon ground pepper |
| 2 | cups peeled, diced potato |
| 2 | cups milk |
| 1 | cup light cream |
| 2 | tablespoons flour |
| | salt to taste |
| 1 | pound fresh or frozen fish steaks, cut into 3/4-inch chunks |
| 1 | tablespoon butter |

1. In a large pot, cook bacon until crisp. Remove bacon, reserving 1 table-spoon of drippings in the pot. Drain bacon on paper towels and crumble.
2. Add fish stock or chicken broth, onions, pepper, and potatoes to the drippings. Bring to a boil. Reduce heat and cook until potatoes are tender. Break up potatoes slightly with a fork.
3. Combine milk, cream, flour, and salt. Mix until smooth.
4. Add to the potato mixture and cook and stir until slightly thickened. Add fish, turn down heat, and simmer until fish flakes, 3 to 5 minutes.
5. Stir in butter. Top each serving with crumbled bacon bits.

**Variations**

Try adding 6 ounces of shrimp with the fish.

To make clam chowder, substitute 13 ounces minced clams for the fish and clam juice for the fish stock.

# Home Place Inn Seafood Chowder

This seafood chowder was so good I had to ask for the recipe. Glenda Burt, the proprietor of The Home Place Inn on Prince Edward Island, was kind enough to share it with *The Charlottesville Collection* and me.

| | |
|---|---|
| 4 | medium potatoes |
| 24 | ounces haddock fillet |
| 1 | cup diced lobster meat |
| 2 | cups water |
| 1/2 | cup butter |
| 1/2 | cup finely diced onion |
| 2/3 | cup finely diced celery |
| 1 1/3 | cups flour |
| 3 | quarts milk |
| 6 1/2 | ounces canned chopped clams, undrained |
| 1/2 | teaspoon black pepper |
| 2 | teaspoons white pepper |
| 2 | teaspoons salt |
| 1 | teaspoon dried tarragon |

1. Peel and cook potatoes. Drain and dice.
2. Cook haddock and lobster in 2 cups water over medium heat for a few minutes, until tender. Reserve liquid.
3. In a large pot, melt butter over medium heat, add onion and celery, and sauté for 5 minutes.
4. Stir in flour. Cook a few minutes and slowly whisk in milk.
5. Add haddock, lobster, seafood liquid, clams with juice, and seasonings.
6. Bring to a slow boil and remove from heat. Adjust seasonings to taste.

# Tortellini Soup

| | |
|---|---|
| 4 | garlic cloves, minced |
| 8 | ounces cheese tortellini |
| 28 | ounces chicken broth |
| 14 | ounces diced tomatoes |
| 1 | package (12 ounces) frozen spinach, thawed |
| | salt and pepper to taste |

1. Place garlic, tortellini, and chicken broth in a large pot. Boil for 5 to 7 minutes.
2. Add tomatoes and spinach. Simmer for 30 minutes over low heat. Add salt and pepper to taste.


# Cream of Shiitake Soup

| | |
|---|---|
| ¼ | pound fresh shiitake mushrooms |
| ¼ | cup butter |
| 2 | cups chopped onion |
| 3 | tablespoons flour |
| 28 | ounces chicken broth |
| 2 | cups whipping cream |
| ¼ | teaspoon pepper |
| ¼ | teaspoon nutmeg |

1. Remove stems from mushrooms and discard. Chop the caps finely.
2. In a saucepan, melt butter, add onion and mushrooms, and cook until tender.
3. Add flour, stirring vigorously. Gradually add broth, stirring continuously.
4. Stir in cream, pepper, and nutmeg. Remove from heat and serve.

**Yield: 4 to 6 servings**

# Swiss Cheese and Onion Soup

| | |
|---|---|
| 3 | tablespoons butter |
| 4 | cups thinly sliced onion |
| 1/2 | teaspoon minced garlic |
| 2 1/2 | cups beef stock |
| 3 | tablespoons flour |
| 1 1/2 | cups milk |
| 8 | ounces shredded Swiss cheese |
| 1 | tablespoon sherry |
| 1/2 | teaspoon grated horseradish |
| 3/4 | teaspoon dry mustard |
| 1/2 | teaspoon pepper |
| 2 | drops Tabasco |

1. Heat 1 tablespoon of the butter in a skillet and sauté onions and garlic over medium heat until tender. Add stock and let simmer for about 30 minutes.
2. In another pan, heat remaining 3 tablespoons of the butter. Whisk in flour and cook over medium heat for 1 minute. Whisk in 3/4 cup of the milk and let it start to thicken, then add the remaining milk and stir vigorously until thickened. Add cheese, sherry, horseradish, mustard, pepper, and Tabasco and stir well until blended.
3. Add the onion mixture to the cheese sauce and mix well.

# Hearty Vegetable Beef Soup

With a good loaf of bread or rolls, this makes a great main meal.

| | |
|---|---|
| 1 | pound uncooked beef, cut into $1/2$-inch cubes |
| 1 | tablespoon vegetable oil |
| $1/2$ | cup chopped onion |
| $1/2$ | cup small carrots |
| $1/2$ | cup chopped celery |
| $1/4$ | cup red wine |
| $1/2$ | cup V-8 or tomato juice |
| 14 | ounces canned diced tomatoes |
| $1/2$ | teaspoon pepper |
| | salt to taste |
| 1 | pint water |
| 16 | ounces beef broth or water |
| 2 | teaspoons bouillon granules |
| $1/4$ | cup pearl or quick-cooking barley |
| 20 | ounces frozen mixed vegetables or 3 cups assorted vegetables |
| 2 | cups $1/2$-inch cubes potato |

1. Brown beef in oil in a large pot.
2. Add onion, carrots, celery, wine, juice, tomatoes, pepper, salt, water, broth, and bouillon. If using pearl barley, add it with the water.
3. Cover and boil gently for about 1 hour, adding water if necessary for desired consistency.
4. Add mixed vegetables, quick-cooking barley, and potatoes. Cook another 15 minutes, until the vegetables are tender. Season to taste.

# Pumpkin Soup

|   |   |
|---|---|
| 1 | cup chopped onion |
| 2 | tablespoons butter |
| 5 | ounces Rotel tomatoes and chilies |
| 28 | ounces chicken broth |
| 29 | ounces canned pumpkin |
| 1/2 | teaspoon nutmeg plus additional for garnish |
| 1 1/2 | cups milk or cream |
|   | sour cream for garnish |

1. In a skillet, sauté onion in butter until translucent.
2. In a blender, puree tomatoes and chilies. Add onion and puree.
3. Transfer to a large soup pot and add broth, pumpkin, and nutmeg. Let simmer for 20 minutes.
4. Stir in milk or cream. Heat through.
5. Serve with a dollop of sour cream and a sprinkle of nutmeg.

**Yield: 6 to 8 servings**

# Zesty Beef and Potato Soup

|   |   |
|---|---|
| 1/2 | pound lean ground beef |
| 2 | cups peeled, cubed, uncooked potato |
| 1/2 | cup chopped onion |
| 12 | ounces tomato sauce |
| 2 | cups beef broth |
| 1 | teaspoon ground pepper |
| 10 | ounces diced Rotel tomato and chilies |
|   | salt to taste |

1. In a skillet, cook ground beef, separating as it cooks.
2. Combine all ingredients in a soup pot and simmer for 45 minutes.
3. Taste and add salt if desired.

# Quick Onion Soup

| | |
|---|---|
| 3 | cups sliced onion |
| 2 | tablespoons butter |
| 1 | tablespoon sugar |
| 2 | tablespoons flour |
| 1/8 | teaspoon thyme |
| 1/2 | teaspoon salt |
| 1/4 | teaspoon ground pepper |
| 28 | ounces canned beef broth |
| 4 | slices French bread, toasted |
| 3/4 | cup shredded Monterey Jack |

1. Place onion and butter in a 2-quart bowl. Cover and microwave at high 4 to 6 minutes.
2. Stir and microwave at high about 6 minutes more.
3. Combine sugar, flour, and seasonings. Mix with 1 cup of the broth. Microwave at high 2 minutes.
4. Stir and add to onions. Add remaining beef broth. Microwave at high 4 to 6 minutes. Stir well.
5. Pour into bowls and top each with toasted French bread. Sprinkle with cheese and place under broiler until melted.

**Yield: 4 servings**

# Cabbage Soup

This is low in calories, delicious, and a cinch to make. It's even good without butter.

| | |
|---|---|
| 2 | teaspoons butter |
| 1 1/2 | cups thinly shredded green cabbage |
| 1 | clove garlic, finely chopped |
| 1/2 | cup coarsely chopped onion |
| 1/2 | cup coarsely chopped carrot |
| 4 | cups chicken broth |
| 1/2 | teaspoon ground pepper |
| 1/2 | teaspoon caraway seed |
| 3 | tablespoons fresh parsley |
| | salt to taste |

1. In a large saucepan, melt butter and add cabbage, garlic, onion, and carrot. Sauté for 5 minutes over medium heat.
2. Add broth, pepper, and caraway.
3. Cover and cook slowly for about 15 minutes, until the vegetables are tender. Sprinkle in parsley. Add salt if desired.

**Yield: 2 to 4 servings**

**Note**

This recipe may be doubled or tripled, but I don't recommend freezing the result.

# Basic Bean Soup

- 1/2   cup chopped celery
- 1/2   cup chopped onion
- 1   clove garlic, crushed
- 1/2   cup chopped green peppers
- 1/2   pound diced ham or bacon
- 1   tablespoon olive oil
- 16   ounces crushed tomatoes
- 1/2   cup dried beans (kidney, pinto, split peas, navy, or black), soaked, drained, and rinsed
- 1   tablespoon basil
- 1/4   teaspoon ground pepper
- 1/4   teaspoon cumin
- 16   ounces beef broth
- 2   cups water
-   salt to taste

1. Sauté celery, onion, garlic, green peppers, and bacon (if using) in oil over medium heat.
2. Combine all ingredients in a large pot.
3. Cook slowly for 2 hours, until all is tender. Add more water if necessary.

**Note**

This is a good way to use leftover ham of any kind. I put extra cold cuts in the freezer for just such uses.

**Variation**

If more zip is desired, add one can (10 ounces) of Rotel tomatoes and chilies, diced; 1 teaspoon hot sauce; or 1 to 2 chopped jalapeños.

# Lentil Soup with Beef

| | |
|---|---|
| 1/2 | **pound dried lentils** |
| 4 | **cups water** |
| 1 | **tablespoon olive oil** |
| 1 | **cup chopped onion** |
| 1/2 | **teaspoon minced garlic** |
| 1 | **cup chopped celery (include leaves)** |
| 1/2 | **cup chopped carrots** |
| 2 | **cups chopped tomatoes** |
| 3 | **cups beef broth** |
| 1/2 | **cup chopped parsley** |
| 1/4 | **pound beef, cut into 1/4-inch pieces** |
| 1/2 | **teaspoon ground pepper** |
| 1 | **jalapeño, chopped fine (optional)** |

1. Wash lentils and boil in water for 15 minutes or soak for 2 hours. Drain and set aside.
2. Heat oil in a large saucepan and sauté onion and garlic for 5 minutes over medium heat.
3. Add all ingredients and cook slowly for 30 to 45 minutes.

## Note

This is a good way to use up leftover steak.

# Lentil Soup with Ham

| | |
|---|---|
| 1/2 | pound lentils |
| 1 | quart water |
| 1 | cup chopped onion |
| 3/4 | teaspoon crushed garlic |
| 1 | tablespoon olive oil |
| 1 | cup cubed or chopped ham |
| 1/2 | cup chopped carrots |
| 1/2 | cup chopped celery |
| 1/2 | cup chopped parsley |
| 2 | cups diced tomatoes |
| 1/2 | teaspoon cumin |
| 1/2 | teaspoon coriander |
| 1/2 | teaspoon ground pepper |
| 2 | tablespoons lemon juice |

1. Soak lentils in 1 quart of water for 2 hours or boil for 15 minutes. Drain and set aside.
2. Sauté onion and garlic in oil over medium heat for 3 minutes.
3. In a large saucepan, combine all ingredients except lemon juice, stirring well. Cook over medium heat about 1 hour, until all is tender.
4. Add lemon juice and stir well.

# Carrot and Coriander Soup

| | |
|---|---|
| 1 | cup sliced onion |
| 2 | tablespoons butter |
| $1/2$ | teaspoon crushed garlic |
| 1 | teaspoon ground coriander |
| $1^1/3$ | pounds carrots, peeled and sliced |
| $1/4$ | pound potatoes, peeled and sliced |
| 5 | cups chicken stock |
| $1^1/4$ | cups fresh orange juice |
| $2/3$ | cup heavy cream |
| | salt to taste |
| $1/2$ | teaspoon ground pepper |

1. In a soup pot, cook onion in butter over medium heat until soft. Stir in garlic and coriander and cook for 2 minutes.
2. Add carrots, potatoes, stock, and orange juice. Cook for 25 to 30 minutes, until carrots and potatoes are soft.
3. Puree the soup in a blender and return to the soup pot. Stir in cream and season with salt and pepper.

**Yield: 8 to 10 servings**

# Homemade Tomato Soup

This family favorite is a world apart from canned tomato soups.

|   |   |
|---|---|
| 1 | cup chopped onion |
| 1/2 | teaspoon minced garlic |
| 1 | tablespoon butter |
| 1 | tablespoon olive oil |
| 32 | ounces canned tomatoes with juice |
| 1/4 | cup finely minced fresh parsley |
| 1/2 | teaspoon dill weed |
| 1/4 | teaspoon ground pepper |
| 2 | teaspoons sugar |
| 2 | cups water or milk |
| 1 | tablespoon vegetable stock granules |
|   | salt and pepper to taste |

1. In a large saucepan, sauté onion and garlic in butter and olive oil over medium heat. Transfer to another container and set aside.
2. In a blender, process tomatoes until smooth. Pour half of the tomatoes into the saucepan. Add onion mixture, parsley, dill, pepper, and sugar to the blender and process until smooth.
3. Return all to saucepan. Add water or milk (see note) and vegetable stock granules and simmer over low heat for 40 minutes. Add salt and pepper to adjust taste.

**Note**

Do not be alarmed if, when you add milk, it curdles a bit. Let it simmer and it will be fine.

# Cauliflower-Cheese Soup

| | |
|---|---|
| 2 | cups peeled diced potato |
| 2 | cups cauliflower pieces |
| 1 | cup chopped carrot |
| $1/2$ | teaspoon minced garlic |
| 1 | cup chopped onion |
| $1^1/2$ | teaspoons salt |
| 2 | cups water or chicken stock |
| $1^1/2$ | cups grated Cheddar |
| 2 | cups milk |
| $1/4$ | teaspoon dill weed |
| $1/4$ | teaspoon ground caraway seed |
| $1/4$ | teaspoon dry mustard |
| $1/4$ | teaspoon ground pepper |
| $1^1/2$ | cups cauliflowerets |

1. Place potato, cauliflower, carrot, garlic, onion, salt, and water or chicken stock in a pot and cook over low heat for 40 minutes. Let cool slightly and puree in a blender or food processor until well chopped but not smooth.
2. Return to pot and whisk in the remaining ingredients, adding cauliflowerets last.
3. Let simmer until cauliflowerets are tender. Do not boil.

# Jean's Corn Chowder

| | |
|---|---|
| 1¹/₂ | cups diced potatoes |
| ¹/₂ | cup sliced onion |
| 1 | cup chicken broth |
| 1 | tablespoon butter |
| 2¹/₂ | tablespoons flour |
| 1³/₄ | cups milk |
| 1 | pound shoe peg corn, frozen |
| 1 | teaspoon soy sauce |
| ¹/₂ | teaspoon ground pepper |
| | salt to taste |

1. In a saucepan over medium heat, cook potatoes and onion in broth until tender.
2. Combine butter and flour and microwave at high for 1 minute to make a roux. Add 1 cup of the milk and stir to make smooth. Microwave at high for 2 minutes and stir.
3. Add roux and remaining ingredients to potatoes and cook slowly for about 6 to 8 minutes, stirring well. Season to taste.

The Albemarle Pippin was a popular commercial apple produced by grafting a New York apple variety to the native Albemarle crabapple. After Queen Victoria tasted the Albemarle Pippin, brought to her in 1838 by Alexander Stevenson, the Albemarle native who was then American ambassador to Great Britain, she would have no other on her table.

# Beef Barley Soup

| | |
|---|---|
| 1 | pound lean sirloin, trimmed and cut in thin strips |
| $1/2$ | cup chopped onion |
| 2 | medium carrots, sliced |
| $1/2$ | teaspoon crushed garlic |
| 4 | cups beef broth |
| 1 | cup barley |
| 2 | tablespoons chopped fresh parsley |
| $1/2$ | teaspoon salt |
| 1 | teaspoon pepper |
| 14 | ounces canned diced tomatoes |
| 1 | cup fresh or frozen peas |
| 1 | cup fresh or frozen green beans |

1. Combine all ingredients except peas and green beans in a soup pot.
2. Bring to a boil. Reduce heat and simmer for 2 or 3 hours. Add peas and beans and let simmer another 15 minutes. Season to taste. Add water if needed for desired consistency.

### Variations
Other vegetable combinations may be added, but avoid too many strong-flavored vegetables.

# Hearty Minestrone

| | |
|---|---|
| 1½ | cups chopped onion |
| 1 | cup sliced celery |
| 1 | teaspoon minced garlic |
| 2 | tablespoons olive oil |
| 1 | cup sliced carrots |
| 1 | cup sliced potato |
| 1 | cup chopped cabbage |
| 14 | ounces canned diced tomatoes or 2 cups diced fresh tomatoes |
| 6 | cups chicken broth or stock |
| 2 | cups water |
| 1 | cup white wine (optional) |
| ½ | teaspoon ground pepper |
| ¼ | cup chopped fresh parsley |
| ½ | teaspoon dried rosemary |
| ½ | cup peas, fresh or frozen |
| ½ | cup uncooked small macaroni |
| ½ | cup green beans, fresh or frozen |
| 14 | ounces canned red kidney beans |
| 14 | ounces canned chick-peas |
| | salt to taste |
| | Parmesan (optional) |

1. In a large pot over medium heat, sauté onion, celery, and garlic in olive oil for a few minutes, until the onion is just translucent.
2. Add all ingredients except macaroni, green beans, kidney beans, chick-peas, salt, and Parmesan. Bring to a boil. Turn down heat and simmer for 30 minutes.
3. Add remaining ingredients and let simmer another 20 minutes.
4. Serve hot, with Parmesan if desired.

**Variation**
Add 1 can (10 ounces) diced tomatoes and green chilies for more zip.

# Crab Bisque with Spinach

| | |
|---|---|
| 20 | ounces frozen chopped spinach, thawed |
| 2 | cups chicken broth |
| 1 | pound fresh crabmeat |
| 2 | tablespoons butter |
| 1 | cup chopped onion |
| 1/4 | cup chopped celery |
| 1/4 | cup chopped green pepper |
| 2 | tablespoons flour |
| 1 | cup milk |
| 2 | cups heavy cream |
| 1 | teaspoon Worcestershire sauce |
| 1/2 | teaspoon ground pepper |
| 1/4 | teaspoon dried thyme |
| 1/4 | teaspoon dried basil |
| | salt to taste |

1. In a blender, process spinach and chicken broth until smooth.
2. Drain crabmeat and pick out any cartilage.
3. Melt butter in a medium pan and sauté onion, celery, and green pepper over medium heat until soft. Add flour and stir well. Reduce heat to low and stir in milk.
4. Gradually add cream and cook and stir for several minutes. Add seasonings and spinach mixture and stir well. Simmer and stir until thoroughly heated.
5. Stir in the crabmeat and simmer until heated through. Add salt to taste.

**Yield: 6 to 8 servings**

# Cream of Celery Soup

2    cups thinly sliced celery

2    tablespoons water

3    tablespoons flour

1    tablespoon butter

2    cups milk

2    cups chicken broth

1/2   teaspoon dill weed

1/2   teaspoon pepper

1    tablespoon chopped fresh parsley

     salt to taste

1.  Microwave celery and water at high for 4 to 5 minutes. Set aside.

2.  In a measuring cup, microwave flour, butter, and 1/2 cup of the milk
    at medium-high for 2 minutes. Stir with a fork until smooth.

3.  In a saucepan, heat cooked celery, broth, and remaining milk almost to a
    boil. Stir in flour mixture slowly.

4.  Turn down heat. Add dill, pepper, and parsley and simmer for about 10
    minutes. Add salt to taste.

# Edie's Cold Curry Soup

chill 24 hours

What a delicious surprise this was when Edie served it to me!

- 2 tablespoons curry powder
- 2 cups clam juice
- 2 cups orange juice
- 2 cups V-8 juice
  sour cream or yogurt for garnish
  chopped fresh parsley for garnish

1. Heat curry powder in a dry pan, being careful not to burn it.
2. Add juices and bring to a boil. Simmer 5 minutes.
3. Let cool and refrigerate 24 hours (see note).
4. Top with a dollop of sour cream or yogurt and parsley if desired.

**Note**
Refrigerating for 24 hours is an essential step.

# Chilled Cucumber-Yogurt Soup

chill 1 hour

- 4 cups peeled, seeded, diced cucumber
- 2 cups water
- 2 cups plain yogurt
- 1 clove garlic, crushed
- 1 tablespoon honey
- 1½ teaspoons salt
- ½ teaspoon dill weed
- 2 tablespoons chopped fresh chives

1. Puree all ingredients in a food processor or blender.
2. Chill in refrigerator for 1 hour or more, until very cold. Serve.

# Cool Cream of Cucumber Soup

chill 2 to 3 hours

| | |
|---|---|
| 20 | ounces canned cream of celery soup |
| 1 | medium cucumber, peeled and chopped |
| 2 | teaspoons finely chopped parsley |
| 1 | green onion, chopped |
| 2 | cups milk |
| 1/4 | teaspoon dried dill weed |
| 1/2 | teaspoon ground pepper |
| | sour cream for garnish |
| | paprika for garnish |

1. Combine soup, cucumber, parsley, and onion in a blender. Blend until smooth.
2. In a large bowl, combine cucumber mixture with milk and seasonings and chill in refrigerator for several hours.
3. Before serving, top with sour cream and paprika.


# Berries and Wine Soup

| | |
|---|---|
| 3 | pints strawberries, washed, hulled, and halved |
| 1 | cup water |
| 1/4 | cup flour |
| 1/2 | cup sugar |
| 2 | cups red wine |
| 2 | cups orange juice |
| 3 | cups sour cream |
| 1 | cup milk |

1. In a saucepan over medium heat, cook strawberries in water for 10 minutes.
2. In another saucepan, combine flour and sugar. Heat slowly. Stir in wine and orange juice and continue to stir over low or medium heat about 10 minutes, until mixture boils. Add to strawberries and let cool.
3. Puree mixture in a blender. Add sour cream and milk and blend until smooth. Chill before serving.

# Cold Raspberry Soup

| | |
|---|---|
| 20 | ounces frozen raspberries, thawed and drained |
| 1 | cup water |
| 1 | cup cran-raspberry juice |
| $^1/_8$ | teaspoon ground cloves |
| $1^1/_2$ | teaspoons cinnamon |
| $^1/_2$ | cup sugar |
| 1 | tablespoon lemon juice |
| 16 | ounces raspberry yogurt |
| | sour cream for garnish |

1. In a blender, puree raspberries with $^1/_2$ cup of the water.
2. In a saucepan, heat raspberries, cran-raspberry juice, remaining water, cloves, cinnamon, and sugar just to boiling.
3. Strain to remove seeds. Let cool.
4. Add lemon juice and whisk in yogurt. Refrigerate until cold. Serve in small bowls with a dollop of sour cream if desired.

**Yield: 4 to 6 servings**

**Note**
Cold Raspberry Soup will keep for several days in the refrigerator.

# SALADS AND SALAD DRESSINGS

Basil Vinaigrette
Balsamic Vinegar Dressing
Jean's Red Onion Vinaigrette
Sun-Dried Tomato Dressing
Lemon Avocado Dressing
Sesame Dressing
Honey-Walnut Vinaigrette
Raspberry Dressing
Spinach Salad Dressing
Orange Poppy Seed Dressing
Creamy Parmesan Dressing
Quick Russian Dressing

# About Salads and Salad Dressings

Guidelines for good nutrition recommend seven fruits and vegetables a day. Without salads, this standard would be pretty hard to meet. Fortunately, the possibilities are virtually infinite.

For the most part, the recipes below call for fresh vegetables and fruits. A few exceptions enable you to open a can and have a quick meal. The majority of the salads were selected with an eye toward ease of preparation, availability of ingredients, and good flavor. A few more complex recipes have been included because they are unique and exceptional.

I urge you to explore the vinegars, peppers, seaweeds, and tofus that are now readily available and affordable. They add variety and new tastes. Nor should you be afraid to experiment with greens; use endive, arugula, romaine, spinach, radicchio, bok choy, the green and red lettuces, and even mesclun, a mix of greens that is very nutritious. I sometimes cringe when served iceberg lettuce because it has so little nutrition.

More and more, I have been using feta and black olives in salads. I've found that even those who say they don't like black olives enjoy them when they are chopped and mixed with salad dressings and cheese.

Traditional salad dressings have more oil than vinegar. For health reasons, some people prefer to reduce this ratio. The dressings don't taste as smooth, but they are better for you. You have to judge for yourself how important those calories are. Several of the salad dressings here have much less oil than is customary. My oil of choice is olive oil because it is so much more nutritious, but a few salads need canola oil instead. Keep in mind that olive oil solidifies when very cold.

A way of reducing calories in mayonnaise-based salad dressings is to use light mayonnaise or Miracle Whip or similar salad dressings. You can cut calories in prepared mayonnaise and salad dressings by diluting them with plain or vanilla yogurt.

## Quick Fixes

A lovely and nutritious salad can be easily prepared using ingredients at hand in just a few minutes. Simple combinations served on a bed of greens include:

1. Orange sections and chopped pecans
2. Sliced fresh tomatoes, alone or with red onion and/or cucumber
3. Canned pineapple slices, pears, apricots, or peaches with a dab of cottage cheese or cream cheese mixed with maple syrup
4. Cooked shrimp (whether frozen and thawed or freshly prepared) with cocktail sauce
5. Apple slices lightly coated with cinnamon and sprinkled with lemon juice
6. Marinated artichoke hearts with tomatoes and green peppers
7. Feta, chopped black olives, and vinaigrette

# Ivy Inn Wild Mushroom Salad

**The Ivy Inn Restaurant**
*Angelo Vangelopoulos, Chef*

|   |   |
|---|---|
| 3 | ounces each shiitake, portobello, and oyster mushrooms, unwashed |
| 3 | ounces chèvre (goat cheese) |
| 1/4 | cup chopped walnuts, lightly toasted |
| 2 | ounces Virginia Surrey Bacon or other quality smoked bacon |
| 2 | Roma tomatoes |
| 2 | green onions (whites and greens) |
| 1 | tablespoon balsamic vinegar |
| 1/2 | teaspoon Dijon mustard |
| 1/2 | teaspoon minced fresh garlic |
| 1/4 | teaspoon minced shallot |
|   | salt and pepper to taste |
| 5–6 | tablespoons olive oil |
| 2 | tablespoons balsamic vinegar |
|   | handful of baby greens |

1. Remove stems from mushrooms and cut into 1/8-inch-thick slices. Do not wash. Set aside.
2. Divide cheese into 4 equal portions. Roll gently into balls and press into the walnuts to lightly coat. Shape into round, flat medallions about 1/2-inch thick.
3. Slice bacon strips crosswise, 1/8-inch thick. Render slowly over medium heat, until thoroughly cooked and crisp. Set aside.
4. Cut tomatoes through the core into quarters. Lay the pieces flesh-side down and use a sharp knife to remove the membrane and seeds (position the knife parallel to the cutting board and gently slice through the tomato, leaving the flesh intact). Cut into 1/4-inch dice and set aside.
5. Wash green onions thoroughly. Remove root ends and cut on the bias into slices 1/16-inch thick. Set aside.
6. Make the dressing by mixing balsamic vinegar, mustard, garlic, shallot, salt, and pepper in a small bowl. Slowly drizzle in 1 1/2 ounces of the olive oil and whisk briskly to form an emulsion. Season to taste.
7. Preheat broiler.

8. In a large sauté pan, heat remaining olive oil over high heat until smoking.
9. Tilt pan away from you and carefully add mushrooms, being careful not to splash hot oil on yourself. Sprinkle liberally with salt and pepper and let mushrooms start to brown on one side before stirring (see note). Cook for 2 to 3 minutes, stirring only once or twice.
10. Place goat cheese on a baking sheet and put under broiler until warm and lightly toasted.
11. Add tomatoes, bacon, green onions, and walnuts to mushrooms in saucepan and heat through. Deglaze with vinegar, stir vinegar in, and remove from heat.
12. In a salad bowl, lightly toss baby greens with vinaigrette. Divide evenly between four plates. Spoon mushrooms over each pile of greens and top with goat cheese. Serve immediately.

**Yield: 4 servings**

**Note**
Moving the mushrooms too soon or too often will cause them to steam themselves in the pan.

# Parmesan Croutons

| | |
|---|---|
| ¼ | loaf French bread |
| 1½ | tablespoons olive oil |
| 1 | clove garlic, crushed |
| 2 | tablespoons grated Parmesan |

1. Cut the crust from the bread and cube into ½-inch pieces.
2. Heat oil and garlic until slightly browned. Discard garlic and add bread cubes. Sauté until slightly brown and drain on paper towels.
3. In a resealable plastic bag, toss croutons with cheese.

**Note**
These croutons may be stored in the refrigerator for up to 3 days before serving.

# Summer Fruit Salad

|  |  |
|---|---|
| 2 | cups orange sections |
| 1 | cup grapefruit sections |
| 1 | cup seedless grapes |
| 8 | ounces canned pineapple tidbits |
| 1/2 | cup chopped pecans |
| 1 | cup sour cream |
| 1 | tablespoon sugar |
| 1 | teaspoon grated lime rind |

1. Combine fruits and nuts in a bowl.
2. In another bowl, combine the sour cream with sugar and lime rind.
3. Pour the sour cream mixture over the fruit and toss gently.
4. Serve on greens.

**Yield: 6 to 8 servings**


# Cranberry Fruit Salad                    refrigerate overnight

|  |  |
|---|---|
| 1 | cup fresh cranberries |
| 1/4 | cup sugar |
| 1 1/2 | cups miniature marshmallows |
| 1 | cup diced Granny Smith apples |
| 1/2 | cup seedless green grapes, halved |
| 1/4 | cup chopped pecans |
| 1/2 | cup heavy cream, whipped |

1. In a blender, finely chop cranberries.
2. Combine cranberries, sugar, and marshmallows in a bowl. Refrigerate overnight.
3. Combine apples, grapes, and pecans and mix with the cranberry mixture; fold all into whipped cream. Serve.

# Lime Carrot Salad

| | |
|---|---|
| 4 | cups grated carrot |
| 2 | tablespoons olive oil |
| 4 | teaspoons fresh lime juice |
| 1/2 | teaspoon ground cumin |
| 1/4 | teaspoon ground ginger |
| 1/4 | teaspoon ground pepper |
| 2 | cups spinach leaves, torn into pieces |

1. Place carrot in a bowl.
2. In another bowl, combine remaining ingredients except spinach and whisk until well blended.
3. Pour over carrots and mix well. Refrigerate for at least 2 hours or overnight.
4. Serve over spinach leaves.

Yield: 4 servings

# Sophie's Avocado and Grapefruit Salad

| | |
|---|---|
| 1 | large grapefruit |
| 1 | large or 2 small avocados |
| 8 | lettuce leaves |
| 4 | tablespoons vinaigrette dressing |

1. Peel the grapefruit whole and remove the white pith. With a sharp knife, cut the sections from the membranes and remove the seeds.
2. Peel the avocados and slice into crescent-shaped sections.
3. Divide lettuce onto four plates. Alternate sections of grapefruit with slices of avocado atop the lettuce.
4. Drizzle dressing over each salad and serve.

Yield: 4 servings

# Raspberry Gelatin Salad

This is an excellent salad to serve with a heavy meal. It is very refreshing to the palate.

| | |
|---|---|
| 3 | ounces raspberry Jell-O |
| 3/4 | cup boiling water |
| 10 | ounces frozen raspberries in syrup, thawed |
| 8 | ounces canned crushed pineapple |
| 1/4 | cup chopped pecans |
| 1 | cup sour cream |

1. Dissolve Jell-O in boiling water. Stir in raspberries, pineapple, and pecans. Blend well.
2. Spoon 1/2 the mixture into an 8 x 8-inch pan. Chill 2 to 3 hours, until set, keeping remainder at room temperature.
3. Spoon sour cream evenly over set raspberry layer. Spoon remaining raspberry mixture over sour cream. Chill until set.
4. Cut into squares and serve on greens.


# Red Cabbage Slaw

| | |
|---|---|
| 3 | cups shredded red cabbage |
| 1 | red apple, cored and diced |
| 8 | ounces canned crushed pineapple |
| 3 | tablespoons brown sugar |
| 3 | tablespoons vinegar |

1. Combine cabbage and fruit.
2. Add remaining ingredients and mix well.
3. Chill before serving.

# Zippy Tomato Salad

chill 2 to 3 hours

About as nutritious and low-calorie as you can get!

| | |
|---|---|
| ¹/₂ | **cup fresh or frozen peas** |
| 2 | **medium tomatoes** |
| 4 | **tablespoons fresh green chili pepper strips** |
| 1 | **teaspoon lemon juice** |
| 1 | **teaspoon minced parsley** |
| | **lettuce leaves** |

1. Cook peas in the microwave (frozen peas, at high for just a minute or two; fresh peas, in 2 tablespoons of water at high for 3 to 5 minutes).
2. Peel and seed tomatoes and cut into ¹/₄-inch strips.
3. Combine all ingredients. Cover and chill for several hours.
4. Serve on lettuce leaves.

**Yield: 2 to 3 servings**

# Cold Stuffed Tomatoes

Cut off the stem end of a medium or large tomato and scoop out the pulp and seeds with a tablespoon, leaving the outer casing intact. You may want to save some of the seedless pulp to enhance the flavor of the filling or for use in some other salad. It will keep for a day or two in the refrigerator.

Fill the tomato casing with your choice of filling. The possibilities are nearly limitless, but these are particularly successful:

1. Chopped vegetables mixed with a little mayonnaise or yogurt and flavored with herbs (e.g., chives, marjoram, or basil) as desired. Some vegetables, such as green beans, need to be precooked slightly
2. Tuna, chicken, or shrimp salad
3. Chopped egg and sweet pickle mixed with a little mayonnaise

# Green Bean, Walnut, and Feta Salad

1½   pounds green beans
1    cup crumbled feta
1    cup diced red onion
1    cup roasted walnuts, chopped

Dressing:

¼    cup olive oil
½    cup fresh mint leaves
¼    cup white wine vinegar
½    teaspoon minced garlic
½    teaspoon salt
½    teaspoon pepper

1. Wash, stem, and slice green beans lengthwise.
2. Steam beans until crisp-tender. Plunge in cold water and pat dry.
3. Combine beans, feta, onions, and walnuts and toss. Set aside.
4. Blend dressing ingredients in a blender or food processor.
5. Toss salad with dressing shortly before serving.

**Yield: 6 to 10 servings**

# Tomatoes and Mozzarella with Fresh Pesto

2/3 **cup packed fresh basil leaves**

2/3 **cup packed fresh mint leaves**

1/2 **cup packed fresh parsley leaves**

1/3 **cup pine nuts**

1/3 **cup Parmesan**

1/2 **teaspoon fresh rosemary**

1 1/2 **teaspoons crushed garlic**

1/2 **teaspoon salt**

1/2 **cup olive oil**

1 **tablespoon balsamic vinegar**

**freshly ground pepper to taste**

3 **medium vine ripe tomatoes, sliced**

3/4 **pound mozzarella cheese, sliced 1/8-inch thick**

1. First, prepare the pesto (see note). In a blender or food processor, process all but the tomatoes and mozzarella until smooth.
2. On a large platter, arrange the tomato slices alternately with the mozzarella slices in a ring, overlapping slightly.
3. Spoon 1/2 of the pesto in the center of the slices. Use leftover sprigs of herbs as a garnish and serve.

**Note**

Step 1 produces 1 cup of pesto, which may be stored in the refrigerator for up to one week. Bring to room temperature before using.

# Different Vegetable Salad

|     |                                   |
|-----|-----------------------------------|
| 2   | cups broccoli flowerets           |
| 2   | cups cauliflower flowerets        |
| 1   | cup brussels sprouts, halved      |
| 1/2 | cup celery slices                 |
| 1/2 | cup onion slices                  |
| 9   | ounces frozen artichoke hearts    |

Dressing:

|     |                              |
|-----|------------------------------|
| 1/4 | cup tarragon vinegar         |
| 1/4 | cup vegetable oil            |
| 2   | teaspoons sugar              |
| 1/2 | teaspoon prepared mustard    |
| 1/2 | teaspoon minced garlic       |
| 1/2 | teaspoon salt                |

1. In a steamer basket, steam the broccoli, cauliflower, brussels sprouts, and celery until crisp-tender. Do not overcook.
2. Combine dressing ingredients and mix well.
3. In a bowl, combine and gently mix steamed vegetables, onion, and artichoke hearts.
4. Pour dressing over vegetables and marinate overnight.

# Cucumber Salad

| | |
|---|---|
| 1 | cup thinly sliced, peeled cucumber |
| 2 | teaspoons sugar |
| 1 | tablespoon white wine vinegar |
| 1 | teaspoon chopped fresh dill |

1. Put cucumbers in a bowl of ice to crisp for at least 30 minutes.
2. In a cup, dissolve sugar in vinegar. Stir in chopped dill.
3. Pour vinegar mixture over well-drained cucumber slices and stir gently to coat thoroughly.
4. Marinate for at least 3 hours in the refrigerator.
5. Drain off all but a couple of tablespoons of the marinade and serve.

**Variation**

Combine ½ cup thinly sliced onion with cucumbers before preparing.


# Chinese Cucumber Salad

| | |
|---|---|
| 4 | cucumbers, sliced |
| 2 | teaspoons salt in 2 cups cold water |
| 4 | tablespoons red wine vinegar |
| 4 | tablespoons soy sauce |
| 4 | tablespoons sugar |
| 4 | teaspoons sesame oil |
| 1 | teaspoon Tabasco |

1. Soak cucumber slices in saltwater for 30 minutes. Drain.
2. Combine remaining ingredients and pour over cucumbers. Let stand for at least 30 minutes.
3. Drain off half the liquid before serving.

# Cabbage Salad

- **3**    **cups shredded cabbage**
- **$2/3$**    **cup sliced red onion**
- **$1/2$**    **cup grated carrots**
- **$1/2$**    **cup sliced celery**
- **$1/2$**    **cup thinly sliced green pepper**

Dressing:
- **$1/4$**    **cup oil**
- **$1/2$**    **cup sugar**
- **$1/2$**    **cup vinegar**
- **$1/2$**    **teaspoon dry mustard**
- **$1/2$**    **teaspoon celery seed**
- **$1/8$**    **teaspoon hot sauce**

1. Combine vegetables in a large bowl.
2. Combine dressing ingredients in a blender or food processor and process until well blended.
3. Pour dressing over cabbage mixture and refrigerate for an hour or more before serving.

# Elegant Potato Salad

| | |
|---|---|
| 2 | pounds potatoes (approximate) |
| 1/4 | cup white wine vinegar |
| 1/4 | cup canola oil |
| 2 | tablespoons lemon juice |
| 2 | tablespoons sugar |
| 1/2 | cup mayonnaise |
| 1/2 | cup chopped shallots or onion |
| 1/2 | cup sliced celery |
| 1/2 | cup chopped cucumber |
| 2 | tablespoons minced fresh parsley |
| 1 | tablespoon finely snipped fresh dill |
| 1/4 | cup chopped sweet pickle |
| 2 | eggs, hard-boiled, shelled, and diced |

1. Scrub potatoes and boil until just tender. Drain, let cool slightly, peel, and dice. Transfer to a bowl.
2. Combine vinegar and oil and pour over potatoes while they are still warm.
3. While potatoes are cooling further, combine lemon juice, sugar, and mayonnaise. Fold into the potatoes.
4. Add remaining ingredients and toss gently.
5. Refrigerate for a couple of hours to let flavors mix.

# Spinach Salad

|     |                                        |
|-----|----------------------------------------|
| 3   | slices bacon                           |
| 4   | cups shredded spinach                  |
| 1/2 | cup thinly sliced onion                |
| 2   | eggs, hard-boiled, shelled, and sliced |
| 1/2 | cup sliced mushrooms                   |
| 1   | tablespoon sugar                       |
| 1/2 | teaspoon ground pepper                 |
| 4   | tablespoons balsamic or wine vinegar   |
| 2   | tablespoons bacon fat or olive oil     |
|     | salt to taste                          |

1. Microwave bacon in a covered dish at high for 2 minutes.
2. Place spinach in 2 to 4 individual serving bowls and add onion. Top with eggs and mushrooms.
3. Crumble bacon on top of the salads.
4. Mix sugar, pepper, vinegar, and oil or warm bacon fat together until well blended. Pour over each salad and serve.

**Yield: 2 large, entrée-size salads or 4 side salads**

**Variations**

Use Spinach Salad Dressing (page 98) instead of bacon fat/olive oil mixture.

Fresh herbs, such as rosemary or thyme, may be added to vary the flavor.

# Greek Salad

5    cups torn mixed greens

1    cup sliced red onion

¼    cup ¼-inch slices green onion

6    radishes, thinly sliced

3    tablespoons olive oil

¼    teaspoon dried oregano or 1 teaspoon freshly chopped oregano

3    tablespoons red wine vinegar

3    ounces feta

½    cup sliced black olives

    anchovies (optional)

1. Combine greens, onions, and radishes.
2. In a jar, combine olive oil, oregano, and vinegar. Shake well.
3. Toss dressing with salad. Top with feta, olives, and anchovies, if desired.

**Yield: 4 to 6 servings**

# Red Beet Salad
marinate 24 hours

3    tablespoons sugar

3    whole cloves

3    whole allspice or ¼ teaspoon ground allspice

¼    cup red wine vinegar

16    ounces canned beets, sliced into strips

3    tablespoons drained prepared horseradish

    fresh parsley for garnish

1. In a saucepan, simmer sugar, spices, and vinegar for 5 minutes.
2. Place beets in a refrigerator bowl and gently stir in horseradish.
3. Pour sauce over all.
4. Cover and marinate for 24 hours in the refrigerator.
5. Drain and decorate with parsley before serving.

**Note**

This will keep for a week in the refrigerator.

# Pasta Salad with Radicchio and Blue Cheese

A favorite of blue cheese lovers.

| | |
|---|---|
| 3/4 | pound pasta shells or penne |
| 2 | tablespoons olive oil |
| 3/4 | cup milk (2% or richer) |
| 1/4 | pound blue cheese |
| 1/2 | teaspoon salt |
| 1/2 | teaspoon ground pepper |
| 3 | tablespoons chopped onion |
| 1 | head radicchio, washed and separated into leaves |
| 1/3 | cup walnuts, chopped and toasted |

1. Cook pasta according to package directions. Drain well.
2. In a large bowl, toss pasta with olive oil.
3. Combine milk, blue cheese, salt, pepper, and onion in a blender or food processor and blend. Pour over pasta.
4. Serve pasta on radicchio leaves and sprinkled with nuts.

**Yield: 6 to 8 servings**

# Sandy's Rotelle Salad

This salad is great for picnics and covered-dish suppers. I've seen people who say they don't like ripe olives come back for seconds!

| | |
|---|---|
| 2 | pounds rotelle |
| 6 | ounces pitted black olives, chopped |
| 1/2 | pound pepperoni, finely chopped |
| 1/2 | pound Parmesan, grated |
| 1/2 | pound feta, crumbled |
| 1 1/2 | teaspoons dried basil |
| 1/2 | teaspoon fresh ground pepper |
| 1/2 | cup olive oil |
| 1/2 | cup red wine vinegar |

1. Cook pasta until just tender, being careful not to overcook. Drain.
2. Combine olives, pepperoni, Parmesan, and feta in a bowl. Stir in seasonings and oil and vinegar.
3. Add pasta and mix gently until well coated.

**Yield: 10 to 14 servings**

On July 4, 1826, the day Thomas Jefferson died, Henry Martin was born a slave at Monticello. For fifty-three years, he rang the bells (since replaced by electric chimes) that marked the time at the University of Virginia. During his tenure, only one day passed without the sound of Martin's bells—after Lee surrendered to Grant at Appomattox, UVa students turned the bell over and filled it with water, which froze and cracked it.

# Penne Pasta and Spinach Salad

| | |
|---|---|
| 8 | ounces penne |
| 1/4 | cup lemon juice |
| 1/4 | cup cider vinegar |
| 1/4 | cup olive oil |
| 2 | teaspoons coarsely ground pepper |
| 1/2 | teaspoon salt |
| 1/2 | cup slivered, roasted red pepper |
| 2 | cups washed, dried, 1/2-inch strips of fresh spinach |
| | whole leaves endive or other lettuce |
| 1/2 | cup walnuts |

1. Cook pasta in salted water about 12 minutes, until al dente. Drain and rinse with cold water to stop cooking.
2. In a bowl, combine lemon juice, vinegar, olive oil, pepper, and salt and whisk vigorously. Mix in roasted peppers. Pour over pasta and marinate 30 minutes.
3. Toss pasta mixture and spinach. Serve on lettuce or endive, topped with walnuts.

**Yield: 6 to 8 servings**

# Pork Fruit Salad

$1/2$   pound lean pork, cooked and sliced into $1/4$-inch strips

$1/2$   cup seedless green grapes, halved

$1/2$   cup sliced grapefruit

$1/2$   cup sliced strawberries

  2   tablespoons orange juice

  1   tablespoon red wine vinegar

  1   teaspoon canola oil

  1   tablespoon honey

$1/2$   teaspoon Dijon mustard

$1/2$   teaspoon poppy seed

      lettuce to cover 2 salad plates

1. In a bowl, toss pork and fruit.
2. In another bowl, combine orange juice, vinegar, oil, honey, mustard, and poppy seed and mix well. Pour over fruit and pork and marinate 10 to 20 minutes.
3. Drain off any extra juices and serve on greens.

**Variations**

Several different fruits are delicious with pork. Use kiwi, orange, pear, or whatever is available.

If you're in a hurry, use a prepared salad dressing.

# Ham and Spinach Salad

This is a summer supper on the run—just serve it with bread or rolls.

| | |
|---|---|
| 2 | cups washed, dried, torn fresh spinach |
| 1 | egg, hard-boiled, shelled, and sliced |
| 2 | ounces boiled ham, thinly sliced and cut into $1/2$-inch strips |
| $1/2$ | cup frozen peas, thawed |
| $1/2$ | cup shredded Monterey Jack |
| $1/4$ | cup thinly sliced onion |
| $1/4$ | cup mushrooms pieces, washed |

1. Combine all ingredients in a salad bowl and toss.
2. Serve with Caesar, Italian, or vinaigrette dressing.

**Variation**
Substitute bacon for the ham.

# Orange Chicken Salad                                    chill 1 to 2 hours

| | |
|---|---|
| $1/2$ | cup diced celery |
| $1/2$ | cup thinly sliced green pepper |
| 1 | cup orange sections, seeded |
| 2 | cups cooked, diced chicken |
| $1/4$ | cup mayonnaise |
| $1/4$ | cup plain yogurt |
| $1/4$ | teaspoon salt |
| 2 | tablespoons orange juice |
| 2 | tablespoons honey |
| $1/2$ | cup almonds, slivered |
| $1/4$ | teaspoon poultry seasoning |

1. Combine celery, green pepper, and oranges in a large bowl. Add chicken.
   In another bowl, combine remaining ingredients and mix well to make dressing.
2. Combine chicken mixture and dressing and refrigerate until chilled.

**Yield: 4 to 6 servings**

# Curried Chicken Salad

| | |
|---|---|
| 1 | cup pineapple tidbits |
| 1/2 | cup grapes, halved |
| 1/4 | cup water chestnuts, sliced |
| 1/2 | cup chopped celery |
| 1/2 | cup almonds, slivered and toasted |
| 1/2 | cup mayonnaise |
| 1 | teaspoon curry powder |
| 2 | teaspoons soy sauce |
| 2 | teaspoons lemon juice |
| 2 | cups cooked, cubed chicken |

1. Combine pineapple, grapes, water chestnuts, celery, and almonds in a large bowl.
2. In a small bowl, combine mayonnaise, curry powder, soy sauce, and lemon juice.
3. Combine pineapple mixture, mayonnaise mixture, and chicken and chill for several hours.

**Yield: 4 to 6 servings**

# Chicken Salad with Fruit

Served with a baguette or roll, this is another easy and complete meal.

| | |
|---|---|
| 1/2 | cup pineapple chunks or tidbits |
| 1/2 | cup seedless grapes, halved |
| 1/4 | cup sliced celery |
| 1 1/2 | cups cooked, cubed chicken |
| 1 | tablespoon plain yogurt |
| 2 | tablespoons salad dressing (e.g., Miracle Whip) |
| 1/4 | cup pecans, chopped |

1. Combine fruits, celery, and chicken in a bowl.
2. Mix yogurt and dressing in a cup.
3. Combine mixtures gently. Sprinkle with nuts and serve.

# Chicken, Pasta, and Spinach Salad

chill 1 to 2 hours

This is a great salad that's a full meal.

| | |
|---|---|
| 4 | **ounces elbow macaroni** |
| 1/2 | **cup snow peas** |
| 1/2 | **cup water** |
| 3 | **cups cooked, cubed chicken breast** |
| 1 | **cup grapes, halved** |
| 2 | **cups torn fresh spinach** |
| 1 | **cup sliced celery** |
| 1 | **cup diced cucumber** |
| 2 | **green onions, sliced** |

1. Cook macaroni according to package directions, until just tender.
2. In a saucepan over medium heat, simmer snow peas in water for 2 minutes. Drain. Let cool.
3. Combine peas, pasta, and remaining ingredients and refrigerate until chilled.
4. Serve with your favorite vinaigrette dressing and a baguette.

**Yield: 4 servings**

# Country Club Grilled Chicken and Spinach Salad

| | |
|---|---|
| 1/2 | teaspoon salt |
| 1/4 | teaspoon ground pepper |
| 1/2 –1 | pound chicken breasts |
| 1 | pound spinach |
| 1/4 | cup vinaigrette dressing |
| 1 | tablespoon honey |
| 1/2 | teaspoon prepared mustard |
| 1/2 | cup walnuts, chopped |
| 1/2 | cup seedless grapes |

1. Salt and pepper chicken breast and grill. Slice into 1/4 x 4-inch strips.
2. Wash, stem, dry, and slice spinach into 1-inch strips.
3. Combine vinaigrette, honey, and mustard in a food processor and blend. Add chopped walnuts.
4. Mound spinach on 4 plates. Arrange warm chicken slices on top. Top with grapes and vinaigrette dressing and serve immediately.

**Yield: 4 servings**

# Curried Shrimp and Rice Salad

| | |
|---|---|
| 2 | tablespoons lemon juice |
| 1/2 | cup mayonnaise |
| 1 | teaspoon curry powder |
| 2 | cups cooked rice, cooled |
| 1/2 | cup chopped fresh parsley |
| 4 | tablespoons Italian dressing, vinaigrette type |
| 2 | ripe avocados |
| 1/2 | cup chopped celery |
| 1/2 | cup ripe or stuffed olives, sliced |
| 2 | cups shrimp, cooked, deveined, and well chilled |

1. Combine lemon juice, mayonnaise, and curry. Mix well and refrigerate for 10 to 20 minutes.
2. Toss rice with parsley and 2 tablespoons of the Italian dressing.
3. Peel and slice the avocados. Coat with remaining 2 tablespoons of Italian dressing.
4. Shortly before serving, combine celery, half of the olives, shrimp, and curried mayonnaise.
5. Assemble the dish with the rice on the bottom. Heap shrimp mixture on top and surround with sliced avocados. Sprinkle with remaining olives and serve.

### Variation

Substitute 1 cup crabmeat for 1 cup shrimp to make a curried seafood salad.

# Beef Stir-Fry Salad

| | |
|---|---|
| 1 | pound tender beef strips |
| 1 | tablespoon plus 1/4 cup olive oil |
| 1/4 | teaspoon salt |
| 1/4 | teaspoon pepper |
| 2 | tablespoons balsamic vinegar |
| 1–2 | tablespoons Dijon mustard |
| 1 | clove garlic, crushed |
| 1 | teaspoon honey |
| 3 | cups washed, torn salad greens |
| 1/2 | cup croutons |
| | Parmesan to pass |

1. Sauté beef strips in 1 tablespoon olive oil for 3 to 5 minutes, until lightly browned. Season with salt and pepper. Turn out on paper towels.
2. In a small bowl, whisk together 1/4 cup olive oil, vinegar, mustard, garlic, and honey until well blended.
3. Toss salad greens and dressing. Divide onto plates and arrange beef strips and croutons on top. Pass the Parmesan.

**Yield: 4 servings**

# Cold Beef Salad

$1/4$    **cup wine vinegar**

$1/4$    **cup pickle juice**

$1/2$    **cup canola oil**

$1/2$    **teaspoon salt**

$1/2$    **teaspoon ground black pepper**

1    **tablespoon Dijon mustard**

2    **tablespoons chopped fresh parsley**

$1 1/2$    **pounds cold cooked roast beef, trimmed of fat and cut into $1/2$-inch strips or thinly sliced**

1    **cup thinly sliced red onion**

     **small head of leaf lettuce**

     **Parmesan Croutons (page 70; optional)**

1. Mix vinegar, pickle juice, oil, salt, pepper, mustard, and parsley in a blender or food processor.
2. Put beef and onion in a bowl and pour marinade over. Store in the refrigerator for 4 to 6 hours.
3. Drain marinade and discard.
4. Serve beef and onion on a thick bed of broken lettuce. Add croutons if desired.

**Note**

This is easy to prepare ahead of time.

**Variation**

Substitute leftover pork for the roast beef.

# Roasted Shallot Vinaigrette

**Copper Mine Restaurant, Wintergreen Resort**
*Michael Miles, Chef*

| | |
|---|---|
| 1/3 | cup shallots |
| 2 2/3 | cups olive oil |
| 1 | pint balsamic vinegar |
| 1/2 | teaspoon freshly ground black pepper |
| 4 | teaspoons finely chopped chives |
| 2 | teaspoons finely chopped basil |
| 4 | teaspoons finely diced pimentos |
| 1 | teaspoon salt |
| 1/2 | tablespoon Dijon mustard |

1. Preheat oven to 350 degrees.
2. Place shallots in a shallow baking pan and sprinkle with some of the olive oil. Roast in oven until tender, 10 to 20 minutes. Peel and chop.
3. Combine all ingredients in a mixing bowl and mix well. Let sit for a while to let flavors mix.


# Basil Vinaigrette

chill 1 hour

| | |
|---|---|
| 1 1/3 | cups olive oil |
| 2/3 | cup white wine vinegar |
| 1/4 | cup chopped fresh basil |
| 2 | green onions, finely chopped |
| 1/2 | teaspoon salt |
| 1/2 | teaspoon pepper |

1. Blend or whisk together all ingredients.
2. Cover and refrigerate until chilled.

## Note

Basil Vinaigrette is especially good on tomato salads.

# Balsamic Vinegar Dressing

let stand 1 hour

- ¹/₂ cup balsamic vinegar (see note)
- ¹/₄ cup virgin olive oil
- 1 teaspoon finely chopped fresh basil
- ¹/₂ teaspoon finely chopped fresh oregano
- ¹/₄ teaspoon freshly ground pepper

1. Combine all ingredients in a bottle or jar.
2. Let sit at least 1 hour before serving. Will keep for a week.

## Note

Balsamic vinegar is made from Trebbiano grapes harvested near Modena, Italy, and aged in barrels for 2 to 40 years—the longer the better. It has a mellow vinegar flavor.

## Variations

Vary the herbs used in this recipe. Dill and celery seed lend another taste. When I'm in a hurry, I use 1 teaspoon herbes de Provence.

# Jean's Red Onion Vinaigrette

refrigerate overnight

- ¹/₂ medium red onion, sliced
- ¹/₂ cup canola oil
- ¹/₂ cup sugar
- ¹/₄ cup vinegar
- 1 teaspoon salt
- 2 tablespoons water

1. Place all ingredients in a food processor and process until well blended.
2. Refrigerate overnight.

# Sun-Dried Tomato Dressing

chill 1 hour

| | |
|---|---|
| 12 | slices sun-dried tomato |
| 1/3 | cup balsamic vinegar |
| 1 | tablespoon tomato paste |
| 1 | teaspoon chopped garlic |
| 1 | teaspoon dried oregano |
| 1/8 | teaspoon black pepper |
| 1/2 | cup olive oil |
| 1/4 | teaspoon salt |

1. Soak tomatoes in water until soft.
2. Combine all ingredients in a blender and blend well.
3. Let stand in refrigerator at least 1 hour before serving.


# Lemon Avocado Dressing

| | |
|---|---|
| 1 | medium ripe avocado |
| 2 | tablespoons fresh lemon juice |
| 1/4 | teaspoon crushed garlic |
| 1/2 | cup sour cream |

1. Peel, halve, and pit avocado.
2. Combine all ingredients in a blender or food processor and blend until smooth.

**Note**

This dressing is especially good on fruit salads.

# Sesame Dressing

chill 2 to 3 hours

| | |
|---|---|
| 1/3 | cup white wine vinegar |
| 1 | cup canola oil |
| 1 | teaspoon sesame oil |
| 1/3 | cup sugar |
| 1/4 | cup soy sauce |
| 1/4 | cup chopped onion |
| 1/2 | teaspoon crushed garlic |
| 2 | teaspoons sesame seeds |

1. Combine all ingredients in a blender and blend until well mixed.
2. Refrigerate for several hours before serving.

# Honey-Walnut Vinaigrette

chill 1 to 2 hours

| | |
|---|---|
| 1/3 | cup vegetable oil |
| 3 | tablespoons red wine vinegar |
| 2 1/2 | tablespoons Dijon mustard |
| 1/2 | cup honey |
| 2 | tablespoons water |
| 1/3 | cup walnuts, toasted and chopped |

1. Whisk together or blend in a blender or food processor all ingredients except walnuts.
2. Add walnuts. Cover and refrigerate for an hour or so to let flavors blend.

# Raspberry Dressing

¼   cup cran-raspberry juice

¼   cup seedless raspberry jam

3   tablespoons raspberry vinegar

2   tablespoons olive oil

½   teaspoon salt

¼   teaspoon ground pepper

1. Blend or whisk together all ingredients.
2. Cover and refrigerate until chilled.

**Note**

This is especially good on watercress, endive, or arugula.

# Spinach Salad Dressing                                chill 2 to 3 hours

⅔   cup canola oil

¼   cup red wine vinegar

2   teaspoons lemon juice

2   teaspoons soy sauce

1   teaspoon sugar

1   teaspoon mustard

½   teaspoon curry

½   teaspoon salt

½   teaspoon pepper

¼   teaspoon garlic powder

1. Place all ingredients in a blender or food processor and blend.
2. Before serving, refrigerate for a couple of hours to let flavors blend.

# Orange Poppy Seed Dressing

chill 2 hours

- ¹/₂ cup plain yogurt
- ¹/₂ tablespoon honey
- ¹/₂ teaspoon dry mustard
- ¹/₂ tablespoon thawed frozen orange juice concentrate
- ¹/₂ teaspoon poppy seeds
- 2 drops hot pepper sauce
- ¹/₂ teaspoon grated orange zest

1. Whisk ingredients together.
2. Refrigerate for at least 2 hours before serving. Will keep for about a week.

# Creamy Parmesan Dressing

chill 2 to 3 hours

- ³/₄ cup light Miracle Whip or mayonnaise
- ¹/₄ cup light sour cream
- 2 teaspoons cider vinegar
- ¹/₂ teaspoon crushed garlic
- ¹/₄ cup grated Parmesan

1. Stir all ingredients together in a bowl. If too thick, add a little water.
2. Refrigerate, covered, for at least several hours and up to 2 weeks.

# Quick Russian Dressing

- 1 cup salad dressing (e.g., Miracle Whip) or mayonnaise
- 3 tablespoons catsup
- 2 tablespoons sweet pickle relish

1. Combine all ingredients in a small bowl.
2. Use immediately or refrigerate for up to a week.

# BEEF, PORK, HAM, AND LAMB

# About Freezing Meats

Many recipes in this section will yield 4 to 8 servings. Extra portions of most dishes may be frozen for several months and reheated in the microwave or oven. Exceptions are dishes with crispy vegetables, which will become soft on thawing. Though the vegetables will taste the same, their texture will change. Stir-fries especially are not as good frozen.

If a little frost accumulates on frozen meats, as sometimes happens, rinse it off quickly and blot with a paper towel. That way, you will not get any added flavor from the freezer. I even rinse and blot bread sometimes.

Leftover steak was a particular challenge until I discovered the value of cutting the meat into thin slices before freezing it in resealable bags. Use as much as desired in sauces or in sandwiches.

Another good meat to have in the freezer is ground beef. I buy one of the lean mixes and freeze it in patties in aluminum foil. Doing so has several advantages. If the meat is to be used as hamburger, it is already in patties and easy to separate. If it will be used in a casserole, it can easily be defrosted in the microwave (after removing the aluminum foil), then mixed with the other ingredients or crumbled for spaghetti sauce or chili.

A slice of ham in the freezer provides the flavor for scrambled eggs at breakfast, chef's salad at lunch, or entrée at supper. Another favorite use for ham in my family is in scalloped potatoes (variation, page 216).

# Tuscan Rib Steaks with Gorgonzola Cream

**Rococo's**
*Stuart L. Rifkin, Owner*

| | |
|---|---|
| 4 | 12-ounce rib-eye steaks |
| 2 | teaspoons kosher salt |
| 2 | tablespoons crushed pink peppercorns |
| 1 | tablespoon chopped shallots |
| 1/4 | cup marsala, sherry, or red wine |
| 4 | ounces Gorgonzola or blue cheese |
| 1/2 | cup heavy cream |
| 1 | teaspoon chopped fresh Italian parsley |

1. Rinse steaks and pat dry. Sprinkle salt and pepper on one side of each.
2. On your grill, broiler, or stove, cook steaks over high heat to desired doneness.
3. Sauté shallots in wine over low heat until they are golden brown or the moisture is gone. Add cheese and cream and cook over moderate heat, stirring often, until cheese melts and mixture starts to bubble. Add parsley.
4. Spoon sauce over steaks and serve with mashed potatoes, fresh asparagus, and a hearty California zinfandel or Italian Barolo.

**Yield: 4 servings**

# Pan-Asian Pork Loin

**Northern Exposure**
*Stuart L. Rifkin, Owner*

This is best with basmati or jasmine rice, sugar snap peas sautéed in hot oil with shiitake mushrooms, and a glass of cold beer.

| | |
|---|---|
| 2 | pounds center-cut pork loin |
| 1/4 | cup olive oil |
| 1 | tablespoon chopped fresh parsley |
| 2 | tablespoons chopped fresh basil |
| 1 | tablespoon Chinese five-spice powder |
| 1 | tablespoon kosher salt |
| 1 | teaspoon black pepper |
| 1 | tablespoon minced fresh garlic |
| 1/2 | cup rice wine vinegar |
| 1 | tablespoon finely chopped fresh ginger |
| 1/2 | cup soy sauce |
| 1 | tablespoon molasses |
| 1 | tablespoon brown sugar |

1. Preheat oven to 475 degrees.
2. Rinse pork loin and pat dry. Brush with olive oil.
3. Mix parsley, basil, five-spice powder, salt, and pepper. Coat the sides and ends of the pork loin with the mixture.
4. Place in oven for 5 minutes. Turn heat down to 275 degrees and cook an additional 15 minutes, until the internal temperature reaches 145 degrees. Remove from oven and let stand 10 minutes.
5. Sauté garlic in vinegar over moderate heat until garlic begins to brown. Add ginger, soy, molasses, and brown sugar and cook over low heat until sugar dissolves and sauce begins to bubble.
6. Slice pork into pinky-width slices and arrange on a plate. Spoon sauce over and serve.

**Yield: 4 servings**

# Meatloaf

$^1/_4$     cup tomato catsup plus additional for topping

$^1/_4$     cup chopped tomatoes or tomato juice

$^1/_4$     teaspoon salt

$^1/_4$     teaspoon black pepper

$^1/_8$     teaspoon cayenne

1     egg, lightly beaten

$^1/_2$     cup Italian bread crumbs

$^1/_4$     cup chopped onion

1     teaspoon prepared Dijon mustard

$^1/_2$     cup chopped fresh parsley or 1 tablespoon dried parsley

1     pound lean ground beef

     chili sauce (optional)

1. Preheat oven to 350 degrees.
2. In a large bowl, combine all ingredients except beef and chili sauce. Add beef and gently mix. Line a loaf pan with aluminum foil. Press the mixture firmly into the pan.
3. Spread chili sauce or additional catsup over the top if desired. Bake for 1 hour.

## Notes

Why is a puzzle to me, but almost every man I've encountered loves meatloaf.

Freeze leftover meatloaf in a plastic bag with wax paper between each slice. Reheat defrosted slices by placing them on a covered plate and microwaving for 1 to 2 minutes.

## Variation

Press mixture into greased muffin tins. Cover with foil and bake for 10 minutes at 350 degrees. Remove foil, top with catsup, and bake another 5 to 10 minutes, depending on the size of the muffin tins. Freeze extras in a bag for future meals.

# Barbecued Baby Beef Ribs

| | |
|---|---|
| 2 | pounds baby beef ribs |
| 1 | lemon, thinly sliced |
| 1 | onion, thinly sliced |
| 1/2 | cup catsup |
| 2 | tablespoons lemon juice |
| 1/4 | cup brown sugar |
| 1/8 | teaspoon Tabasco |
| 1/2 | teaspoon dry mustard |
| 1/2 | cup water |
| 1/8 | teaspoon freshly ground black pepper |
| 2 | tablespoons Worcestershire sauce or soy sauce |

1. Preheat oven to 450 degrees.
2. Wipe ribs with a wet towel. Place in a single layer in a shallow roasting pan.
3. Roast ribs with bony side up for 10 minutes. Turn over. Place slices of lemon and onion on the meaty side and roast another 20 minutes. Remove from oven and drain off fat.
4. Combine all other ingredients in a bowl. Brush half the mixture on the ribs and return ribs to oven for about 20 minutes. Baste with more of the catsup mixture.
5. Heat any remaining catsup mixture in the microwave and serve on the side for dipping.

## Note

Extra ribs may be refrigerated for 4 or 5 days, but mine always get eaten well before then.

# Beef and Broccoli Stir-Fry

| | |
|---|---|
| 1 | pound flank steak |
| 2 | tablespoons soy sauce |
| 2 | tablespoons sherry or dry white wine |
| 1 | teaspoon sugar |
| 2 | teaspoons cornstarch |
| 2 | tablespoons olive oil |
| 1 | cup coarsely sliced onion |
| 1 | cup sliced mushrooms |
| 1 | cup broccoli flowerets |
| 2–3 | cups cooked rice |

1. Slice steak, across the grain, into thin strips.
2. In a small bowl, mix soy, sherry, sugar, and cornstarch. Add steak and marinate for at least 1 hour. Drain and reserve marinade.
3. In a skillet over medium-high heat, combine 1 tablespoon of the olive oil, onion, mushrooms, and broccoli and stir-fry for 2 to 3 minutes. Remove to a bowl.
4. In the same skillet, heat the remaining tablespoon of oil. Stir-fry steak strips over medium-high heat for 2 minutes. Add marinade and vegetables and cook for 1 to 2 minutes, until cornstarch cooks and coats vegetables.
5. Serve over rice.

**Variations**

Substitute pork or chicken strips for flank steak.

# Steak Rollup with Noodles

| | |
|---|---|
| 1 | pound lean top round steak |
| 1 | teaspoon chopped fresh thyme |
| 1 | teaspoon chopped fresh sage |
| 1 | teaspoon chopped fresh basil |
| | white butcher's string |
| 2 | tablespoons vegetable oil |
| 14 | ounces canned diced tomatoes |
| 16 | ounces tomato paste |
| 1½ | teaspoons chili powder |
| 1 | cup finely chopped onion |
| ½ | teaspoon salt |
| ¼ | teaspoon ground pepper |
| ¼ | cup chopped fresh parsley |
| 3 | cups cooked noodles |

1. Pound steak into a 6 x 10-inch rectangle about ½ inch thick.
2. Rub with thyme, sage, and basil. Roll up tightly and tie with white butcher's string.
3. In a large frying pan with a lid, over high heat, brown the beef roll on all sides in the oil.
4. Combine remaining ingredients and pour over meat roll. Reduce heat and simmer, covered, for 1 hour. Add a little extra water if all the liquid has evaporated.
5. Remove roll to a cutting board. Cut strings and remove. Slice roll into 8 pieces and serve with noodles.

# Easy Meat Sauce

| | |
|---|---|
| 1/2 | pound lean ground beef |
| 15 | ounces marinara or other tomato-based pasta sauce |
| 1/2 | teaspoon onion powder |
| 1/4 | teaspoon garlic powder |
| 2 | tablespoons grated Parmesan or Romano |

1. Crumble beef into a hot skillet over high heat and separate as it browns. Pour off any fat.
2. Reduce heat and add sauce, seasonings, and Parmesan. Let simmer for 5 minutes.
3. Serve with spaghetti or other pasta.

### Variation

For more zest, add chopped onion, chopped mushrooms, and a chopped hot pepper to the skillet as the meat is browning.

# Beef Barbecue

| | |
|---|---|
| 1 | pound lean ground beef or thinly sliced beef |
| 1/2 | cup chopped onion |
| 1 | teaspoon minced garlic |
| 1 | cup catsup |
| 1 1/2 | teaspoons chili powder |
| 1 1/2 | tablespoons brown sugar |
| 2 | tablespoons vinegar |
| 2 | teaspoons Worcestershire sauce |
| 1/4 | teaspoon ground celery seed |

1. Crumble beef into a hot skillet and brown over high heat. Separate meat with a spatula or spoon.
2. Turn heat down and add onion. Cook until translucent. Add remaining ingredients and simmer about 10 minutes, until thick.
3. Serve on rolls or pitas.

**Yield: 4 servings**

# Greek-Style Beef Stew

The recipe for Greek-Style Beef Stew has been passed down through many generations of Melanie Carrat's family. The dish was served regularly at her grandparents' restaurant, The Plaza Grill, on West Main Street in Charlottesville during the 1930s and '40s.

| | |
|---|---|
| $1/4$ | cup olive oil (see note) |
| $1 1/2$ | pounds stew beef, precut into pieces 1-inch thick |
| 3 | garlic cloves, quartered |
| 3 | medium onions, quartered |
| $3/4$ | teaspoon salt |
| $3/4$ | teaspoon pepper |
| 1 | bay leaf |
| 1 | tablespoon dried oregano |
| 1 | tablespoon dried basil |
| 2 | cups $1/2$-inch-thick celery slices |
| 2 | cups $1/2$-inch-thick carrot slices |
| 3 | medium unpeeled potatoes, cut in small wedges |
| $48 1/2$ | ounces canned whole tomatoes |

1. Heat olive oil in pressure cooker on medium-high and lightly brown beef, garlic, and onions. Add salt, pepper, bay leaf, oregano, basil, vegetables, and tomatoes.
2. Close pressure cooker and cook according to appliance directions for 20 minutes.

**Note**

Because the cost of olive oil in the '30s was prohibitive relative to that of vegetable or other oils, olive oil was not used in the original recipe.

# Beef Stroganoff

| | |
|---|---|
| 1/2 | pound rib or top sirloin steak |
| 1/3 | cup coarsely chopped onion |
| 1 | cup fresh mushrooms, sliced |
| 1 | clove garlic, crushed |
| 1 | tablespoon butter |
| 2 | tablespoons flour |
| 1/2 | cup hot water |
| 1/2 | tablespoon beef bouillon granules |
| 1/4 | teaspoon freshly ground black pepper |
| 1/2 | cup sour cream or low-fat yogurt |
| 1 1/2 | cups cooked noodles |
| 2 | tablespoons chopped parsley (optional) |

1. Trim fat from steak and slice, across the grain, into thin strips. Set aside.
2. Spray a nonstick skillet with vegetable oil and heat over medium-high heat. Add steak, onion, mushrooms, and garlic. Turn down heat and cook until meat is tender, beginning next step in the interim.
3. Put butter and flour in a Pyrex measuring cup and microwave at high for 30 seconds. Add water, bouillon, and pepper. Whisk and microwave at high for 1 minute.
4. Add microwaved mixture to skillet and stir in sour cream or yogurt. Serve over hot noodles and garnished with parsley.

# Basic Beef Stir-Fry

| | |
|---|---|
| 1 | pound rib or sirloin steak |
| 1 | teaspoon olive oil |
| 1 | medium onion, quartered |
| 1 | bell pepper, slivered |
| 1/4 | pound snow peas |
| 2 | teaspoons cornstarch |
| 1/2 | cup bouillon |
| 2 | tablespoons soy sauce |
| 3 | tablespoons sherry (optional) |
| 2 | cups cooked Chinese noodles, rice, or pasta |

1. Trim steak well and slice, across the grain, into thin strips. In a skillet over high heat, brown in the oil.
2. Add onion, peppers, and peas. Turn down heat and cook vegetables until crisp-tender.
3. Dissolve cornstarch in bouillon and slowly stir into skillet mixture. Add soy sauce and sherry and stir again. Serve over Chinese noodles, rice, or pasta.

**Note**
Best when freshly prepared.

**Variations**
Other vegetables, such as mushrooms, celery, or broccoli, may substitute or be added. Mixed frozen vegetables come in several combinations that work well with the basic ingredients in this beef stir-fry.

# Meatballs

Meatballs are another of those staple foods that freeze well and are handy on a busy day. They can be combined with canned pasta sauce and pasta for a quick main meal and are good in barbecue, sweet and sour, and sour cream sauce (variations, page 114). They can also be served as appetizers when you're entertaining.

| | |
|---|---|
| 1 | pound lean ground beef |
| 1 | large egg, beaten |
| 1/2 | cup bread crumbs |
| 1/4 | cup milk |
| 1/4 | cup finely chopped onion |
| 1 | tablespoon dried or 3 tablespoons finely chopped fresh parsley |
| 3/4 | teaspoon salt |
| 2 | teaspoons Worcestershire sauce |

1. Preheat oven to 400 degrees.
2. Combine all ingredients in a bowl and mix thoroughly with your hands.
3. On a piece of wax paper, pat into a rectangle about 3/4-inch thick. Cut into equal portions with a large knife. Roll each portion into a ball and place on a greased baking pan.
4. Bake for 8 to 12 minutes, depending on size of balls. Toss into pasta sauce or store in plastic bags in the freezer for future use.

## Note
Meatballs can be fried in a pan a few at a time, but baking them in the oven all at once is quicker and easier.

## Variations
If more Italian flavor is desired, add 1 clove garlic, crushed, and 1/2 teaspoon oregano. If a spicier flavor is desired, add a chopped hot pepper.

# Sauces for Meatballs

## Spaghetti Sauce

A large variety of spaghetti/tomato-based sauces are available already prepared. Of course, homemade sauces are best.

| | |
|---|---|
| 1 | pound lean ground beef |
| 3/4 | cup chopped onion |
| 1 | tablespoon crushed garlic |
| 1/2 | cup chopped green pepper |
| 1 | tablespoon olive oil |
| 1/2 | teaspoon ground pepper |
| 2 | tablespoons minced, seeded jalapeño |
| 2 | 28-ounce cans crushed tomatoes |
| 12 | ounces tomato paste |
| 1 | teaspoon dried basil |
| 1/2 | teaspoon dried thyme |
| 1 | teaspoon dried oregano |
| 1 1/2 | cups water |
| 2 | tablespoons sugar |
| | salt to taste |

1. In a large pot over medium-high heat, cook beef, onion, garlic, and green pepper in olive oil until meat is browned and onion translucent.
2. Add remaining ingredients except salt and simmer, partially covered, for 3 hours. Stir occasionally and add more water as needed.
3. Add salt to taste and more seasonings as desired.

**Yield: about 2 quarts**

## Pineapple Sweet and Sour Sauce

| | |
|---|---|
| 1 | cup pineapple juice |
| 1 | tablespoon catsup |
| 1 | tablespoon cornstarch |
| 1 | tablespoon brown sugar |
| 1 | tablespoon vinegar |
| 1 | tablespoon soy sauce |

1. Combine all ingredients and cook slowly over low heat until slightly thickened.
2. Add about 20 meatballs and simmer for an additional 20 minutes. Serve.

## Swedish Sour Cream Sauce

| | |
|---|---|
| 1 | cup thinly sliced onions |
| 1 | tablespoon butter |
| 1 | tablespoon flour |
| 1/2 | cup bouillon or beef broth |
| 1/4 | teaspoon cardamom (optional) |
| 1/4 | teaspoon nutmeg |
| 1 | cup sour cream |

1. In a saucepan, sauté onions in butter over medium heat until onion is translucent but not browned.
2. Stir in flour. Add bouillon or beef broth, cardamom, and nutmeg. Cook, stirring well, until thickened.
3. Stir in sour cream and heat through. Add about 40 meatballs and simmer for 20 minutes.

**Note**
Served with noodles, this makes a wonderful entrée.

# Slow-Cook Pot Roast

Meats toughen when cooked at high temperatures. Pot roast cooked just below the boiling point becomes very tender. Cooking in a Crock-Pot is best, but you can also use a big pot over low heat on the stovetop. Or, wrap your roast and some vegetables and spices in aluminum foil and cook in a 250-degree oven for 6 to 10 hours.

# Puff Pastry Beef Triangles

| | |
|---|---|
| 1 | pound lean ground beef |
| 1 | cup chopped onion |
| 12 | ounces beef gravy |
| 1 | teaspoon Worcestershire sauce |
| 1/2 | teaspoon thyme |
| 1 1/2 | cups frozen vegetable mixture, thawed |
| 2 | sheets frozen puff pastry, thawed |

1. Preheat oven to 400 degrees.
2. Cook beef and onion in a skillet over medium heat until browned and separated. Pour off any fat.
3. Add gravy, Worcestershire sauce, and thyme and mix well. Stir in vegetables.
4. Unfold pastries and roll each sheet into a 1-foot square. Cut four 6-inch squares from each.
5. Place 1/2 cup of the meat mixture in the center of each square. Moisten the edges and fold to triangle shapes. Press edges with a fork to seal.
6. Bake on cookie sheets for 25 minutes.

**Yield: 8 servings**

# Ten-Minute Meatloaf

|   |   |
|---|---|
| 1 | pound lean ground beef |
| 2 | eggs, slightly beaten |
| 1/2 | cup bread crumbs |
| 1/4 | cup milk |
| 2 | tablespoons onion soup mix |
| 1/4 | cup catsup |

1. Combine all ingredients and press into a round loaf about 1½ inches thick. Place in a microwavable bowl and cover with plastic wrap, leaving a vent.
2. Microwave at high for 6 to 8 minutes. Drain off liquid.
3. Let stand 10 minutes before slicing.

**Yield: 4 to 6 servings**


# Sloppy Joes

|   |   |
|---|---|
| 1 | pound lean ground beef |
| 1/2 | cup chopped onion |
| 1/2 | cup chopped green pepper |
| 1/2 | cup catsup |
| 1 | tablespoon Worcestershire sauce |
| 1 | teaspoon chili powder |
| 1 | tablespoon brown sugar |
| 1 | tablespoon cider vinegar |
| 1/4 | teaspoon ground pepper |
| 2–4 | drops hot sauce (optional) |

1. In a skillet over medium heat, brown meat. Add onion and green pepper and cook for 2 to 3 minutes, until tender.
2. Add remaining ingredients and heat through.
3. Stir well and serve on a hamburger bun.

# Make-Ahead Chimichangas

| | |
|---|---|
| 1 | pound cooked chicken, pork, or beef |
| 16 | ounces medium or mild salsa |
| 16 | ounces refried beans |
| 1 | can (4½ ounces) green chilies, diced and undrained |
| 1 | ounce taco seasoning |
| 8 | ounces Monterey Jack |
| 16 | 8-inch flour tortillas |
| | salsa for garnish |
| | sour cream for garnish |

1. Shred the cooked meat. Combine in a cooking pan with salsa, beans, chilies, and seasoning. Heat over medium heat and mix well.
2. Cut cheese into 16 half-inch sticks.
3. In a hot, dry skillet, heat tortillas one at a time, about 30 seconds on each side. Remove and place ⅓ cup of the meat mixture in the center, top with a cheese stick, and roll up, tucking the sides in.
4. Place chimichangas in a plastic bag and freeze up to 6 months.
5. To prepare to serve, wrap frozen pieces in aluminum foil and heat in oven for 50 minutes at 350 degrees. Remove foil and bake another 10 minutes. Serve with salsa and sour cream on chopped lettuce.

## Notes

Frozen chimichangas may also be prepared in the microwave. Cover lightly with a paper towel and cook at medium-high for about 12 minutes.

If only a few like it hot, prepare the meat and salsa mixture in two pans, using 8 ounces mild salsa in one and 8 ounces medium salsa in the other. Be sure to mark the chimichangas so you know which is which!

This is a good way to use leftover meat.

# Pork Stir-Fry

| | |
|---|---|
| 1/2 | pound pork, sliced into strips |
| 2 | tablespoons olive oil |
| 1 | tablespoon sesame oil |
| 1/2 | cup onion quarters |
| 1/2 | cup 1-inch slices celery |
| 1/2 | cup sugar pea pods |
| 5 | ounces canned, sliced water chestnuts |
| 1 | teaspoon sugar |
| 2 | tablespoons soy sauce (approximate) |
| 1 | cup chicken broth |
| 1 | tablespoon cornstarch |
| 2 | cups cooked rice |
| 2 | cups cooked crispy noodles |

1. Sauté pork in olive and sesame oil over medium-high heat until brown. Add onion and celery and cook for 5 to 8 minutes, until tender.
2. Add pea pods, water chestnuts, sugar, and soy sauce. Combine broth and cornstarch and stir into mixture.
3. Let simmer 10 to 15 minutes. Taste and add more soy if desired. Serve with rice and crispy noodles.

**Yield: 4 servings**

# Sweet and Sour Pork

| | |
|---|---|
| 2 | teaspoons olive oil |
| 2 | cups pork strips |
| $1/2$ | cup onion chunks |
| $1/2$ | cup bell pepper strips |
| 2 | cups thawed frozen vegetable mix |
| $1/4$ | cup water |
| $1/2$ | cup pineapple juice |
| 2 | teaspoons cornstarch |
| 2 | tablespoons brown sugar |
| 1 | teaspoon soy sauce (approximate) |
| 3 | tablespoons vinegar |
| $1/4$ | teaspoon minced fresh ginger root (optional) |

1. Preheat a skillet or wok and add oil and pork strips. Stir-fry for 2 minutes over high heat.
2. Turn down heat and add vegetables and water. Let cook about 5 minutes.
3. In a bowl, combine pineapple juice and cornstarch. Blend well. Add brown sugar, soy sauce, vinegar, and ginger root. Pour into skillet over cooking vegetables and simmer for 5 minutes, stirring frequently. Check seasoning and add more soy if desired.

## Variations
Substitute previously made meatballs, chicken, or beef for pork.

# Pork Tenderloin

This moist, well-cooked roast is a family favorite—and so easy!

| 1–1½ | pounds pork tenderloin, boned and trimmed (see note) |
|---|---|
| ½ | teaspoon salt |
| ¼ | teaspoon ground pepper |
| 3 | tablespoons Italian dressing (not fat free) |

1. Preheat oven to 400 degrees.
2. Sear roast in hot skillet for 5 minutes.
3. Place roast on large piece of aluminum foil and sprinkle with salt and pepper. Pour dressing over.
4. Wrap well with the foil, place on a baking pan, and bake for 30 to 45 minutes, depending on size. Meat thermometer should read 160 degrees.

## Note

Pork tenderloins and boned pork loins are very popular and readily available. They consist of solid, nonfatty meat that can be baked in foil with seasonings or roasted in the oven or on the grill. Because pork cooks quickly, it is possible to roast vegetables, such as onions, potatoes, and squash, right along with it. Pork loins also can be rubbed with seasoning combinations; some of these can be found in the chapter on accompaniments (page 267).

## Variation

Substitute fresh or dried herbs in a tablespoon of olive oil for the Italian dressing.

# Pork and Vegetables

| | |
|---|---|
| 1 | tablespoon olive oil |
| 1 | pound lean pork, cubed |
| 1/2 | cup chopped onion |
| 1 | pound green cabbage, finely shredded |
| 3 | medium potatoes, peeled and cubed |
| 1 1/2 | cups beef bouillon or stock |
| 1/2 | teaspoon salt |
| 1/4 | teaspoon ground pepper |
| 1/2 | teaspoon caraway seeds |

1. Heat a heavy skillet and add oil and pork. Over medium-high heat, brown pork on all sides. Add onion and cook until just translucent.
2. Stir in remaining ingredients.
3. Cover and simmer over low heat for 45 minutes.

**Yield: 4 servings**


# Honey-Mustard Pork Tenderloins

| | |
|---|---|
| 1/4 | cup honey |
| 1 | tablespoon Dijon mustard |
| 2 | tablespoons vinegar |
| 2 | boneless pork tenderloins (about 1 1/2 pounds), trimmed |

1. Preheat oven to 350 degrees. Combine honey, mustard, and vinegar in a cup.
2. Place the tenderloins on a broiler pan and coat with about half of the mixture, reserving the rest for basting.
3. Roast tenderloins for 30 to 40 minutes, basting regularly with honey mixture, until meat thermometer registers 160 degrees.
4. If desired, make a gravy of the sauce in the bottom of the broiler pan by adding a little flour and water.

**Yield: 6 to 8 servings**

# Orange Pork Chops

| | |
|---|---|
| 8 | thin pork chops |
| $1/2$ | teaspoon salt |
| $1/2$ | teaspoon ground pepper |
| 1 | tablespoon olive oil |
| $3/4$ | cup chopped onions |
| $1\frac{1}{4}$ | cups orange juice |
| 3 | tablespoons white wine vinegar |
| $1\frac{1}{2}$ | teaspoons chopped fresh thyme |

1. Preheat oven to 350 degrees.
2. Sprinkle chops with salt and pepper. In a skillet over high heat, brown in the olive oil on both sides. Remove chops. Reduce heat and sauté onions in the juices.
3. Place chops, onions, and any juices in a large, flat baking pan. Combine orange juice, vinegar, and thyme and pour over chops.
4. Cover and bake for 45 minutes or more, until meat is tender. Uncover and let sauce thicken.

**Yield: 4 servings**

# Pork Medallions

| | |
|---|---|
| 1 | tablespoon olive oil |
| 1 | pound pork tenderloin medallions, cut into $1/2$-inch slices |
| $1/2$ | teaspoon salt |
| $1/4$ | teaspoon ground pepper |
| $1/2$ | cup chopped onion |
| 1 | cup diced tomatoes |
| 1 | tablespoon chopped fresh basil or 1 teaspoon dried basil |
| $1^1/2$ | cups cooked rice or noodles |

1. Heat a skillet over high heat and add olive oil. Sauté pork medallions in the hot oil a few at a time, removing browned slices to a plate until all are cooked.
2. Turn down the heat. Return all pork to skillet and add remaining ingredients.
3. Simmer until sauce is slightly thickened and pork is well cooked, 10 to 15 minutes. Serve with rice or noodles.

## Variation
I have tried this with pork chops, and the result was very good. Cook chops a little longer, about 30 minutes.

Shadrach Battles planted the row of locust trees that face Court Square. He was paid a quart of whiskey for every tree that lived. Every time one of them showed its first leaves, he is reported to have clapped his hands and shouted, "Another quart saved!"

# Pork Chops with Anjou Pears

| | |
|---|---|
| 20 | ounces canned whole onions |
| 1/2 | cup hot water |
| 1/2 | cup golden raisins |
| 6 | loin pork chops, about 1 inch thick, trimmed |
| 1/2 | teaspoon salt |
| 1 | teaspoon Lawry's lemon pepper marinade |
| 3 | tablespoons brown sugar |
| 1/2 | cup sherry |
| 3 | medium Anjou pears |
| 1 | tablespoon cornstarch |
| 1 | tablespoon cold water |
| 6 | maraschino cherries |

1. Drain onions and reserve liquid. Pour hot water over raisins and let stand 5 minutes. Drain.
2. In a skillet over medium heat, brown trimmed pork chops. Drain fat.
3. Sprinkle chops with salt and marinade. Add raisins, onions, brown sugar, and sherry. Cover, reduce heat, and let simmer about 30 minutes, until tender. Add reserved onion liquid if needed.
4. Peel, core, and quarter pears. Add to skillet and continue to simmer for 10 minutes. Remove chops and pears to a warm platter.
5. Blend cornstarch and water and stir into pan juices. Cook until thickened. Pour over pork chops and pears. Garnish with cherries and serve.

# Ham Pastry Roll

This easy-to-make puff pastry lends itself to many different mixtures and fillings. It's a great way to dress up leftover meats and vegetables. Just don't get the fillings too juicy, or it becomes a mess.

| | |
|---|---|
| 1/2 | package (one sheet) frozen puff pastry, thawed |
| 1 | egg, beaten |
| 1 | tablespoon water |
| 1/4 | cup chopped green onion |
| 2 | tablespoons chopped pimento |
| 1/2 | teaspoon dried oregano |
| 1/2 | pound cooked ham, sliced |
| 1/2 | pound cooked turkey, sliced |
| 1 | cup chopped, packed spinach leaves |
| 4 | ounces Swiss cheese, sliced |

1. Preheat oven to 400 degrees.
2. Unfold pastry sheet on a lightly floured board and roll to a 16 x 12-inch rectangle.
3. Combine egg and water and set aside. Combine onion, pimento, and oregano and set aside.
4. Layer meat, spinach, and cheese on one half of the sheet, along the front of the short side about 1 inch from the edge, so that the roll will be 12 inches wide when rolled.
5. Sprinkle with onion mixture and roll to overlap just a bit at the seam. Pinch the pastry together. Place on a baking sheet with the seam down. Brush with the egg mixture.
6. Bake until golden, about 25 minutes. Let cool for a few minutes before slicing and serving warm.

**Yield: 6 servings**

# Veal Medallions

2   tablespoons flour

$1/2$   teaspoon salt

$1/2$   teaspoon ground pepper

2   teaspoons beef bouillon

2   cups water

3   tablespoons olive oil

1   pound veal medallions

1   cup sliced carrots

$1/2$   cup sliced mushrooms

$3/4$   cup diced tomatoes

3   teaspoons chopped fresh basil or 1 teaspoon dried basil

3   tablespoons chopped fresh parsley

1   cup cream sherry

4   tablespoons grated Parmesan

2   cups cooked rice

1. Combine flour, salt, and pepper in a shallow bowl. Dissolve bouillon in the water.
2. In a skillet over medium-high heat, heat the oil. Coat medallions in flour mixture and place in the hot oil. Turn heat down and brown on both sides.
3. Add carrots, mushrooms, tomatoes, basil, bouillon, and parsley and simmer for 35 minutes. Stir in sherry and cheese and simmer an additional 10 minutes.
4. Serve over rice.

**Yield: 4 servings**

# Gratin of Broccoli and Ham

Serve this casserole with noodles for a great meal.

| | |
|---|---|
| 1/4 | cup flour |
| 2 | cups milk |
| 6 | tablespoons butter |
| 1/2 | cup shredded Parmesan |
| 1/2 | cup shredded Swiss cheese |
| 1/4 | teaspoon ground pepper |
| 4 | cups chopped, cooked broccoli |
| 1/3 | pound cooked ham, coarsely chopped |
| 1/2 | cup coarse bread crumbs |

1. Preheat oven to 375 degrees.
2. In a large skillet over medium heat, combine flour, milk, and 4 tablespoons of the butter and stir continuously until thickened into a roux. Let simmer for 5 minutes over low heat.
3. Add cheeses and pepper and stir well.
4. In a well-greased casserole, combine broccoli and ham. Pour cheese mixture over all. Sprinkle with bread crumbs and dot with remaining 2 tablespoons of butter.
5. Bake for 35 minutes, until bubbly.

# Lamb Kabobs

¹/₂    cup olive oil

2    tablespoons chopped fresh parsley

¹/₂    tablespoon salt

2    teaspoons oregano

1    teaspoon pepper

1¹/₂    teaspoons minced garlic

6    tablespoons fresh lemon juice

3    pounds lamb from the leg, cut into 1¹/₂-inch cubes

3    medium onions, quartered

3    bell peppers, cut into 2-inch pieces

5    Italian tomatoes, halved

8    mushrooms (about 1¹/₂ inches in size)

3    tablespoons olive oil

1. Combine oil, parsley, salt, oregano, pepper, garlic, and 3 tablespoons of the lemon juice. Add lamb cubes and marinate all day or overnight.
2. Drain off the marinade and discard. Alternate lamb and vegetables on skewers. Brush with oil and remaining lemon juice.
3. Grill kabobs, turning as necessary, until lamb is done and vegetables are cooked.

# CHEESE AND EGGS

## About Cheese and Eggs

Eggs and cheeses have been given a bad name because of cholesterol and fat content. To some degree that notoriety is unwarranted. Cheeses and eggs are natural foods that impart nutrition and quality to dishes. It is only with excess consumption that they become detrimental. We are fortunate nowadays to have low-cholesterol eggs and low-fat cheeses. Though I have not had success with fat-free cheeses, I have found reduced-fat cheeses to be quite acceptable for most purposes.

Many of the recipes in this section are for special breakfast dishes. Several are from a wonderful bed-and-breakfast in East Boothbay, Maine. The Five Gables Inn is noted for its exceptional fare, and Chef Mark Kennedy was kind enough to exchange recipes with me when I visited there. I have found the results delicious.

### Tips

1. Use your finger or a spoon to scrape out the egg white that remains in a broken eggshell. A lot is lost if this is not done.
2. After hard-boiling eggs, put the date on them in pencil. That way, they can be returned to the egg bin without guesswork.
3. Freeze extra egg whites or yolks in ice cube trays, then store them in plastic bags.
4. Cheese can be frozen. If you're afraid that a piece of cheese will become moldy, toss it into the freezer in a plastic bag. It will not have quite the same consistency, but it will be fine for cooking and most uses. Cheddar will crumble easily after freezing.

# Mike's Fresh Tomato-Basil Fritatta

| | |
|---|---|
| 4 | ounces Cheddar, grated |
| 1 | tablespoon all-purpose flour |
| 4 | ounces Monterey Jack, grated |
| 6 | eggs, beaten |
| 1 | teaspoon Worcestershire sauce |
| 1/2 | cup half-and-half |
| 1 | medium tomato, chopped |
| 1/4 | cup chopped fresh basil (see note) |

1. Toss Cheddar with flour. Place in a greased pie plate and sprinkle with Monterey Jack.
2. Combine eggs, Worcestershire sauce, and half-and-half. Mix well.
3. Pour egg mixture over cheeses and sprinkle with tomato and basil. Bake at 350 degrees for 35 to 40 minutes.

**Yield: 6 servings**

**Notes**

This fritatta can be made 12 hours in advance of baking.

On one occasion, when I didn't have any fresh basil, I used 3 teaspoons dried basil. The result was delicious; my guests loved it.

---

*Of its advantageous situation for health and society, no remark need be made.*
—**James Monroe**, in an advertisement for Ash Lawn–Highland, which he had to sell because of financial difficulties

# Spinach and Feta Tart

| 1½ | pounds fresh spinach |
|---|---|
| 1 | cup diced onion |
| 3 | tablespoons butter |
| 2 | tablespoons all-purpose flour |
| 1 | cup milk |
| 2 | eggs, well beaten |
| 3–4 | ounces feta, crumbled |
| ⅛ | teaspoon freshly ground pepper |
| 1 | pie shell |

1. Preheat oven to 400 degrees.
2. Wash, stem, dry, and shred spinach.
3. In a skillet over medium heat, sauté onion in butter. Stir in flour.
4. Stir in milk a little at a time as the flour thickens it. Remove from burner.
5. Stir in eggs, feta, and spinach. Add pepper.
6. Pour into pie shell and bake for 30 minutes.


# Edie's Quiche

| 4 | eggs, beaten |
|---|---|
| 8 | ounces mozzarella, shredded |
| 5 | ounces pepperoni, sliced |
| 15 | ounces canned artichoke hearts, drained and quartered |
| 1 | 9-inch pie shell, unbaked |

1. Preheat oven to 350 degrees.
2. In a large bowl, combine all ingredients. Pour into pie shell.
3. Bake 40 minutes.

**Yield: 4 to 6 servings**

**Note**

This dish can be frozen before it is baked. Bake frozen quiche, uncovered, for 50 to 60 minutes.

# Blueberry-Stuffed French Toast

| | |
|---|---|
| 12 | slices French bread, $3/4$ inch thick |
| 8 | ounces cold cream cheese, cut into $1/2$-inch cubes |
| 1 | cup fresh or frozen blueberries |
| 12 | eggs |
| $1/3$ | cup maple syrup |
| 1 | cup milk |

Sauce:

| | |
|---|---|
| 1 | cup sugar |
| 6 | teaspoons cornstarch |
| 1 | cup water |
| 1 | cup blueberries |
| 1 | tablespoon butter |

1. Arrange 6 bread slices in a buttered, 9 x 12-inch glass baking dish.
2. Scatter cream cheese and blueberries over the bread. Top with remaining slices.
3. In a bowl, beat eggs. Mix in syrup and milk.
4. Pour egg mixture over bread dish. Cover with aluminum foil and refrigerate overnight.
5. In the morning, keep covered and bake at 350 degrees for 30 minutes. Remove the foil and bake another 30 minutes, until puffed and golden.
6. To make the sauce, stir sugar, cornstarch, and water together in a small saucepan. Cook over moderate heat until thickened.
7. Reduce heat and stir in blueberries. Simmer until berries burst. Stir in butter.
8. Pour sauce over bread and serve.

# Stuffed French Toast

| | |
|---|---|
| 8 | ounces cream cheese |
| 1/2 | cup walnuts, chopped |
| 2 | teaspoons vanilla |
| 4–6 | slices French bread, 1 1/2 inches thick |
| 2 | cups milk |
| 4 | eggs, lightly beaten |
| 2 | tablespoons butter |

1. Combine cream cheese, walnuts, and 1 teaspoon of the vanilla. Warm in microwave very briefly, until soft.
2. Slit the top of the bread slices and stuff 1 to 2 tablespoons of the cream cheese mixture into each.
3. Combine milk and eggs and remaining one teaspoon of vanilla.
4. Heat butter in a griddle or large skillet over medium heat.
5. Dip each bread slice in the egg mixture to coat and place in the heated skillet or griddle. Cook slowly until golden, turning once.


# Barnyard Omelet

| | |
|---|---|
| 4 | large eggs |
| 2 | tablespoons milk |
| | salt and pepper to taste |
| 2 | teaspoons butter |
| 1/3 | cup cottage cheese |
| 2 | tablespoons finely chopped chives |

1. In a bowl, beat eggs. Add milk, salt, and pepper. Beat for 1 minute.
2. In a heavy frying pan over medium heat, melt butter. Pour egg mixture into pan and cook over medium-high heat for about 2 minutes, until firm on the bottom. Tilt pan and lift egg to allow uncooked portion to run under cooked portion. Cook until all is firm and flip eggs. Turn down heat.
3. Combine cottage cheese and chives and place on one half of the omelet. Fold egg over and heat through. Remove to a heated plate and serve.

# Eggs Sonoma

| | |
|---|---|
| 1/3 | cup seeded, chopped tomato |
| 4 1/2 | ounces canned mild green chilies, chopped and drained |
| 2 | tablespoons finely chopped celery |
| 1 | tablespoon finely chopped onion |
| 1 | tablespoon red wine vinegar |
| 1/2 | teaspoon sugar |
| 1/8 | teaspoon crushed dried rosemary |
| 6 | eggs |
| 1/4 | teaspoon salt |
| 1/8 | teaspoon ground pepper |
| 1 | tablespoon butter |
| 4 | six-inch flour tortillas |

1. In a bowl, combine vegetables, vinegar, sugar, and rosemary.
2. In another bowl, beat eggs. Add salt and pepper. Add vegetable mixture to egg mixture.
3. In a skillet or omelet pan over medium heat, melt butter. Add egg and vegetable mixture.
4. Over medium-high heat, cook for about 2 minutes, until firm on the bottom. Tilt pan and lift egg to allow uncooked portion to run under cooked portion. Cook until all is firm and flip eggs.
5. Heat tortillas and serve a portion of egg in each.

# PASTA, RICE, AND BEANS

# About Pasta

It is hard to know which pasta to use for what purpose. Dried pasta is almost as good as fresh pasta, will keep better, and is less expensive. However, fresh pasta does absorb more sauce and becomes more flavorful. It also cooks faster, so much so that it needs to be watched carefully lest it overcook. Fresh pasta expands less, so use an additional twenty-five percent. I like fresh pasta, fettuccine or linguine especially, with cream sauces. I use dried pasta for spaghetti and chunky salads and sauces. Salads composed of shells, rotelles, or elbows, whether dried or fresh, are easiest to eat.

Whole wheat and vegetable pastas bring different flavors. I like whole wheat pastas, but some of the flavored ones have been a disappointment. I prefer to season with sauces.

Egg noodles technically are not pasta and get soggy when used in place of pasta. They do, however, make a good side dish; I use egg noodles with just butter, parsley, and sometimes cheese when I need a starch.

A teaspoon of olive oil added to pasta as you cook it will keep it from sticking together.

# About Rice

Rice selection has become more difficult, too. Basically, there are four types of rice: short- and medium-grain rice, which is soft and sticky and used in paellas and risotto; long-grain rice, which cooks up fluffy, tender, and separate; brown rice, which takes longer to cook, has a wonderful nutty flavor, and is more nutritious; and converted rice, such as Uncle Ben's, which has B vitamins forced into the kernel before the bran is removed. There is also aromatic rice, such as basmati and arborio, and wild rice, which really isn't rice at all, but the seeds of a long-grain marsh grass grown in the northern Great Lakes area. Instant rice has been cooked and then dried again.

Each type has a slightly different cooking time. Either watch the pot carefully or follow the directions on the package.

# About Beans

Beans are very nutritious and underused in American diets. They are reputedly difficult to digest, but some experts say this is so only because our systems are not accustomed to them. The more beans we eat, the theory goes, the better it gets.

I realized only recently the vast variations in the quality of dried beans. Many have been stored for months or even years and have become very hard and lost nutritive value. Some dried beans will soften if brought to a boil and soaked in the water for an hour. Others are still hard after an hour and need far more soaking. If you know the source and age of your beans, you can use the boiling water method. If the age of your beans is unknown, however, you are safer to soak them for at least 4 hours. I find it simplest to soak mine overnight. Whatever you do, be sure to discard the soaking water and rinse the beans before using them.

Some of the recipes in this chapter produce simple, single-dish meals. Vegetarians and calorie counters who have cut back on meat should appreciate the many vegetarian options, which are noted as such. There are also recipes here suitable for vegans, who consume neither meat nor animal products such as milk or eggs. These too have been noted.

Pasta, rice, and beans all freeze very well. In my house, extra rice is always frozen for later use.

# Pasta Portobello

**Pizza Bella**
*Hernan Franco, Head Chef*

| | |
|---|---|
| ¹/₂ | pound tri-color cheese tortellini |
| 1 | ounce (¹/₂ cup) olive oil |
| 2 | cloves garlic, minced |
| | salt and pepper to taste |
| 1 | portobello mushroom, cubed |
| 2 | ounces (¹/₂ cup) diced red onions |
| 2 | ounces (¹/₄ cup) sliced scallions |
| 2 | ounces (¹/₂ cup) diced red peppers |
| 2 | ounces (¹/₂ cup) diced prosciutto |
| 1 | ounce (¹/₈ cup or 2 tablespoons) white wine |
| 6 | ounces (³/₄ cup) cream |
| 1 | ounce (¹/₄ cup) Parmesan |
| 2 | heaping tablespoons chopped fresh basil |

1. Cook pasta according to package directions.
2. While the pasta is cooking, heat olive oil, garlic, salt, and pepper in a saucepan over medium-high heat. Add vegetables and prosciutto and sauté until vegetables are translucent.
3. Deglaze pan with wine and add cream. Bring to a boil and cook until reduced by half. Remove from heat.
4. Add Parmesan and fresh basil and stir.
5. Toss with tortellini and serve.

**Yield: 2 servings**

# Penne Pasta with Chicken and Mushrooms in a Fresh Basil Cream Sauce

**The St. Maarten Café**
*Michael M. L. Merritt, Sous Chef*

| | |
|---|---|
| 12 | ounces penne pasta |
| 3 | tablespoons butter |
| 10 | ounces boneless, skinless chicken breast, cut into thin strips |
| 2 | cloves garlic, finely minced |
| 4 | ounces mushrooms, sliced |
| 1 | bunch green onions, chopped |
| 1/4 | teaspoon crushed red pepper |
| 2 | tablespoons finely minced basil plus basil leaves for garnish |
| | salt and freshly ground pepper to taste |
| 8 | ounces (1 cup) heavy cream |
| 4 | ounces Parmesan, freshly grated |

1. Cook pasta according to package directions.
2. In a large sauté pan, melt butter over medium-high heat. Add chicken, garlic, mushrooms, green onions, red pepper, and minced basil. Sauté until chicken is cooked thoroughly.
3. Add a pinch of salt and pepper. Add heavy cream and half the Parmesan. Cook to reduce and thicken for about 3 minutes.
4. Toss sauce with pasta. Divide into two large pasta bowls and top with remaining Parmesan and fresh basil leaves.
5. Serve with a mixed greens salad with a light vinaigrette and crusty French bread.

# Shrimp 'n' Feta over Garlic-Parsley Fettuccini

**The Nook Restaurant, On the Historic Downtown Mall**
*Terry Shotwell, Owner*

| | |
|---|---|
| 1/2 | cup chicken broth |
| 1 | tablespoon olive oil |
| 1/2 | cup chopped onions |
| 16 | ounces Italian tomatoes, chopped |
| 2 | teaspoons dried oregano |
| 2 | teaspoons dried parsley |
| 1 | cup white wine |
| 1 | pound garlic fettuccini (Pasta by Valente preferred) |
| 1 | cup crumbled feta |
| 1 | pound cooked shrimp |

1. In a large skillet, combine everything except pasta, feta, and shrimp. Let simmer about 20 minutes, until onions are soft.
2. Cook pasta according to package directions. Drain.
3. Toss pasta with sauce and top with feta and shrimp.
4. Serve with a fresh tossed salad and warm garlic toast.

**Yield: 8 servings**

# Vegetable Stir-Fry Pasta

vegetarian; vegan variation

| | |
|---|---|
| 8 | ounces angel hair or other small pasta |
| 2 | teaspoons olive oil |
| 1/2 | cup sliced carrots |
| 1 | cup thinly sliced onion |
| 1/2 | cup sliced celery |
| 1/2 | cup sliced bell pepper (cut in strips) |
| 1 | cup vegetable broth or bouillon |
| 1/3 | cup soy sauce |
| 2 | teaspoons minced fresh ginger |
| 1 | teaspoon garlic powder |
| 1 | teaspoon sugar |
| 1 | tablespoon cornstarch |
| 2 | cups 1/2-inch-thick slices yellow squash |
| 1/2 | cup sliced mushrooms |
| 2 | cups broccoli flowerets |
| 3 | tablespoons white wine |
| | grated Parmesan (optional; omit for vegan dish) |

1. Cook pasta according to directions on package. Drain and set aside.
2. In a large skillet, heat oil. Add carrots, onion, celery, and bell pepper and sauté over medium heat about 5 minutes, until onion is translucent.
3. Combine broth, soy, ginger, garlic powder, sugar, and cornstarch. Pour into skillet, stirring well.
4. Turn down heat and add squash, mushrooms, and broccoli. Let simmer for 3 to 5 minutes. Add wine and heat another minute, stirring gently.
5. Add pasta to skillet and toss with vegetables. Sprinkle with Parmesan. Heat gently until warm.

**Yield: 4 to 6 servings**

# Lemon and Garlic Pasta

vegetarian; vegan variation

| | |
|---|---|
| 8 | ounces linguine |
| 2 | tablespoons chopped chives |
| 1½ | teaspoons minced garlic |
| 2 | tablespoons butter or vegetable oil (for vegan dish) |
| 2 | tablespoons olive oil |
| ¼ | cup lemon juice |
| ¼ | teaspoon salt |
| 1 | teaspoon ground pepper |
| ⅓ | cup chopped fresh parsley |

1. Cook pasta according to package directions. Drain and keep warm.
2. In a skillet over medium heat, sauté chives and garlic for 1 to 2 minutes in butter and olive oil. Add lemon juice, salt, and pepper and heat through.
3. Pour sauce over pasta. Add parsley and toss gently.
4. Serve immediately.

**Yield: 4 servings**

# Ham, Sugar Pea, and Pasta Toss

This is a one-dish meal in a bowl.

|     |                                      |
| --- | ------------------------------------ |
| 2   | cups penne or shell pasta            |
| 1/2 | cup snap peas, fresh or frozen       |
| 1/2 | cup sliced carrots                   |
| 1/2 | cup water                            |
| 1   | cup cubed, cooked ham                |
| 2   | tablespoons butter                   |
| 1   | teaspoon cornstarch                  |
| 6   | ounces unsweetened pineapple juice   |
| 1/4 | cup grated Parmesan                  |
| 1/4 | teaspoon salt                        |
| 1/4 | teaspoon pepper                      |

1. Cook pasta according to package directions. Drain and keep warm.
2. In a skillet over medium-high heat, cook peas and carrots in the water until crisp-tender, about 10 minutes. Drain and set aside.
3. Sauté ham in butter over medium heat for 3 minutes. In a small dish, combine cornstarch and pineapple juice and stir. Add to ham, stirring, and reduce heat. Add peas and carrots. Let simmer over low heat for about 8 minutes.
4. Toss with pasta. Place in a serving dish and sprinkle with Parmesan, salt, and pepper.

# Penne with Spinach

| | |
|---|---|
| 4 | ounces penne or other small pasta |
| 1 | tablespoon butter |
| 1 | tablespoon olive oil |
| 1/4 | cup very thinly sliced red onion |
| 4 | tablespoons cream |
| 2 | cups sliced spinach |
| 1/4 | cup grated Parmesan |
| 4 | slices bacon, cooked and crumbled |
| | salt and pepper to taste |

1. Cook pasta according to package directions. Drain and return to pot.
2. In a skillet, heat butter and oil over low heat. Add onions and cook slowly until translucent. Add cream. Bring to a boil and add spinach. Let simmer about 3 minutes, stirring well, until spinach is wilted but still bright green.
3. Add skillet contents to pasta and stir to mix. Add Parmesan, bacon, and salt and pepper to taste.

Yield: 4 servings


# Egg Noodle Toss                                         vegetarian

| | |
|---|---|
| 1 | pound egg noodles |
| 4 | tablespoons butter |
| 8 | ounces sour cream |
| 1/4 | cup minced onion |
| 2 | tablespoons chopped fresh parsley |
| 3 | tablespoons finely chopped fresh chives |
| 1/2 | teaspoon minced garlic |

1. Cook noodles according to package directions. Do not overcook. Drain.
2. In a saucepan, combine remaining ingredients and gently bring to a boil. Turn down heat and let simmer for about 5 minutes.
3. Toss noodles with sauce and serve immediately.

# Cottage Cheese and Spinach Lasagne          vegetarian

| 20 | ounces frozen chopped spinach |
|---|---|
| 10–12 | lasagna noodles |
| 2 | eggs, beaten |
| 1 | tablespoon chopped parsley |
| 1/2 | teaspoon dried oregano |
| 1 | teaspoon dried basil |
| 1/4 | teaspoon garlic powder |
| 1 | pint small curd cottage cheese |
| 32 | ounces spaghetti sauce |
| 1 | pound mozzarella, shredded |
| 1/2 | cup grated Parmesan |

1. Preheat oven to 350 degrees. Defrost and press water from spinach.
2. Cook lasagna according to package directions.
3. Combine eggs, parsley, oregano, basil, garlic powder, and cottage cheese. Add spinach and mix well.
4. Put 2 tablespoons sauce in the bottom of a 10 x 15-inch baking pan. Top with half the noodles, one third of the mozzarella cheese, half the cottage cheese mixture, and half the remaining sauce. Repeat, topping off with the remaining mozzarella and Parmesan.
5. Bake for 30 minutes.

**Yield: 8 to 10 servings**

# Manicotti Stuffed with Artichoke Hearts     vegetarian

1¹/₂    cups finely chopped onion

3    tablespoons olive oil

¹/₄–¹/₂    teaspoon crushed garlic

28    ounces canned Italian tomatoes, undrained

salt and pepper to taste

1    tablespoon dried basil

1    tablespoon dried parsley

¹/₂    cup reduced-fat ricotta

¹/₂    cup grated Parmesan plus additional for topping

6    ounces marinated artichoke hearts

1    package (8 ounces) manicotti


1.  Sauté onion in oil for a few minutes over medium heat. Add garlic, tomatoes, salt, pepper, basil, and parsley and cook for 30 minutes. Transfer all to a blender and process until a smooth sauce.
2.  Combine ricotta and ¹/₂ cup Parmesan.
3.  Drain artichokes and reserve marinade. Chop into small pieces. Add chopped artichokes and 3 tablespoons of drained marinade to cheeses and mix gently.
4.  Preheat oven to 400 degrees.
5.  Cook manicotti according to package directions. Drain and let cool on wax paper until cool enough to handle.
6.  Stuff shells with the cheese mixture.
7.  Pour a cup of sauce into a 9 x 9-inch pan. Place stuffed manicotti in a single layer in the pan. Pour remaining sauce over all.
8.  Bake for 25 to 30 minutes, until heated through. Sprinkle with more Parmesan before serving.

# Pasta Shells with Roasted Pepper

**vegetarian and vegan**

- ¹/₂    **pound pasta shells**
- 2    **tablespoons olive oil**
- ¹/₂    **cup thinly sliced roasted peppers**
- 1    **cup sliced fresh spinach**
- 1    **teaspoon coarse pepper**
- ¹/₂    **teaspoon salt**
- ¹/₂    **cup walnuts**
- 2    **tablespoons lemon juice**
- 2    **tablespoons cider vinegar**

1. Cook pasta according to package directions. Drain.
2. In a skillet, simmer oil and roasted pepper. Add spinach, pepper, salt, and walnuts. Heat for 2 minutes over medium heat. Add lemon juice and vinegar.
3. Add spinach mixture to pasta and toss gently until well mixed.

**Yield: 6 to 8 servings**

# Mexican Rice

**vegetarian variation**

- 1    **cup uncooked white rice**
- 1    **tablespoon butter**
- 1    **cup diced tomatoes**
- ¹/₂    **cup chopped onion**
- 1    **small garlic clove, minced**
- 4¹/₂    **ounces diced green chilies**
- 13    **ounces chicken broth or vegetable stock (for vegetarian dish)**

1. In a saucepan, sauté rice in butter over medium heat for 5 minutes, stirring occasionally.
2. In a blender or food processor, combine tomatoes, onion, and garlic. Process until pureed.
3. Add tomato mixture, chilies, and broth to rice and boil gently until most of the liquid has evaporated.
4. Fluff with a fork and serve.

# Fried Rice with Roasted Peppers                  vegetarian

| 1 | cup uncooked rice |
| 1/2 | cup chopped red onion |
| 2 | teaspoons butter |
| 2 | eggs |
| 1/2 | cup chopped, roasted red peppers |
| 1/4 | teaspoon freshly ground pepper |
| 1/4 | teaspoon salt |
| 1 | teaspoon soy sauce plus soy to taste |
| 1/2 | teaspoon sesame oil |
| 1 | cup frozen peas, thawed |

1. Cook rice according to package directions until just tender. Drain and rinse in cold water.
2. In a large frying pan, sauté onion in butter over medium heat until translucent. Add eggs and stir until mixed well. Add red peppers, ground pepper, salt, and soy sauce. Cook over medium heat about 5 minutes, stirring frequently.
3. Add sesame oil and stir. Add rice and stir well. Let simmer for about 5 minutes.
4. Add peas and let simmer another 3 minutes. Taste and add more soy if necessary.

**Yield: 4 servings**

# Yellow Rice

Yellow Rice has always been a favorite in the South.

| | |
|---|---|
| 1 | teaspoon olive oil |
| 1/2 | cup chopped onion |
| 2 | cups chicken broth or vegetable stock (for vegetarian dish) |
| 1 | cup uncooked long-grain rice |
| 1/8 | teaspoon ground turmeric |
| 1 | bay leaf |

1. In a heavy saucepan with a lid, heat the oil and sauté the onion until translucent.
2. Add remaining ingredients. Bring to a boil and cover.
3. Turn down the heat and cook for about 20 minutes, until liquid is absorbed and rice is tender. Remove bay leaf and serve.

Yield: 4 servings

## Variations
This rice can be flavored with saffron, which gives it an aromatic character. If substituting saffron for turmeric, heat a bit of the broth first and stir 4 to 5 pieces of saffron into it. Let it sit for a while to allow the aroma to develop. Then add to the remainder of the broth and proceed.

# Green Rice

|   |   |
|---|---|
| 2 | tablespoons butter |
| 1/4 | cup chopped chives |
| 1/2 | cup chopped parsley |
| 1/4 | cup grated Parmesan |
| 3 | cups cooked long-grain rice |
| 1 | cup chopped almonds |
| 1/2 | teaspoon salt |
| 1/4 | teaspoon pepper |

1. In a large skillet, heat butter over low to medium heat. Add chives and parsley and sauté 1 to 2 minutes.
2. Add Parmesan, rice, and almonds. Season with salt and pepper to taste. Stir well while heating through.

# Cheese Rice Casserole

This is another one-dish meal.

|   |   |
|---|---|
| 1 | cup ricotta |
| 1 | cup Miracle Whip salad dressing |
| 1/4 | teaspoon garlic powder |
| 1/2 | teaspoon ground pepper |
| 1 1/2 | cups shredded Monterey Jack |
| 3 | cups cooked white long-grain rice |
| 1 | cup chopped broccoli |
| 1/2 | cup chopped onions |
| 1 | cup frozen peas |

1. Preheat oven to 350 degrees.
2. In a large bowl, combine ricotta, salad dressing, garlic, pepper, and 1 cup of the Monterey Jack. Mix well.
3. Stir in remaining ingredients and transfer all to a greased casserole.
4. Bake 30 minutes. Top with remaining 1/2 cup Monterey Jack and bake 5 minutes more, until cheese has melted.

# Broccoli Rice Casserole

A meal by itself.

| | |
|---|---|
| 1$^1$/$_2$ | cups uncooked white or brown rice |
| 6 | cups chicken broth or vegetable stock (for vegetarian dish) |
| $^1$/$_2$ | cup butter |
| $^3$/$_4$ | cup finely chopped onion |
| $^1$/$_2$ | cup flour |
| 1 | cup heavy cream |
| | salt and pepper to taste |
| 20 | ounces frozen chopped broccoli |
| $^3$/$_4$ | cup chopped mushrooms |
| $^1$/$_2$ | cup bread crumbs |

1. Preheat oven to 350 degrees. Cook rice in 3 cups of the chicken broth. Drain well.
2. In a skillet, heat butter and sauté onion for just a minute. Stir in flour to make a paste. Stir in cream and remaining 3 cups of broth. Season with salt and pepper and stir until well mixed.
3. In a casserole, combine broccoli, mushrooms, rice, and onion mixture. Mix gently. Top with bread crumbs.
4. Bake for 30 minutes.

# Southern Red Rice

| 32 | ounces whole canned tomatoes, undrained |
|---|---|
| 6 | slices bacon |
| 1/2 | cup chopped onion |
| 1/2 | cup chopped celery |
| 1/4 | cup chopped green pepper |
| 2 | cups uncooked white long-grain rice |
| 1 | teaspoon salt |
| 1/4 | teaspoon pepper |
| 1 | teaspoon sugar |
| 1/8 | teaspoon hot sauce |

1. Preheat oven to 350 degrees.
2. Process tomatoes in a food processor or blender until smooth. Set aside.
3. In a large skillet, sauté bacon until crisp. Remove and drain on paper towels. Drain all but 1 tablespoon of drippings from the skillet.
4. Add onion, celery, and green pepper to the skillet and sauté over medium heat until tender. Stir in uncooked rice, tomatoes, and seasonings. Crumble in bacon.
5. Pour into an ovenproof casserole and bake, covered, for 1 hour.

**Yield: 8 servings**

# Carol's Baked Beans

This is a great dish for picnics or potluck suppers.

| | |
|---|---|
| 84 | ounces high-quality canned baked beans (e.g., Bush or B&B) |
| 8 | strips turkey bacon |
| 1 | cup chopped onion |
| 1/2 | cup chopped green pepper |
| 1 1/2 | cups brown sugar |
| 1/4 | cup butter |

1. Preheat oven to 350 degrees.
2. Remove any pork or visible fat from beans and pour into a baking pan.
3. Microwave turkey bacon until crisp and drain on paper towels, reserving a tablespoon of the fat.
4. Microwave onion and green pepper in reserved bacon fat until tender, at high about 2 minutes.
5. Add brown sugar to beans. Stir in onion mixture and crumbled bacon. Dot with butter.
6. Bake for 1 hour.

On May 24, 1781, the capital of Virginia was moved from Richmond to Charlottesville to escape Cornwallis's British troops. On the night of June 3, British soldiers sent to attack the new capital paused at Louisa County's Cuckoo Tavern, owned by the father of young militia captain Jack Jouett. Jouett, suspecting the soldiers' intent, rode through rough terrain by moonlight to warn the Virginia legislators—Patrick Henry, Thomas Jefferson, James Madison, and three signers of the Declaration of Independence among them.

# Vegetarian Chili

2$^1/_2$   cups dry kidney beans, soaked, drained, and rinsed

1$^1/_2$   cups chopped onion

1$^1/_2$   teaspoons crushed garlic

1   tablespoon olive oil

1   cup chopped celery

1   cup chopped carrots

1   cup chopped green pepper

2   cups chopped fresh tomato

$^1/_2$   cup uncooked brown rice

1   cup tomato juice

2   teaspoons lemon juice

1   tablespoon brown sugar

1   teaspoon cumin

1   tablespoon chopped fresh basil

1–2   tablespoons chili powder (see note)

3   tablespoons tomato paste

3   tablespoons red wine

1. In a large skillet, sauté onion and garlic in olive oil over medium heat until onions are translucent. Add celery, carrots, peppers, and tomato and cook over low heat until tender.
2. Combine all ingredients in a large pot. Heat through and let simmer for 1 hour over low heat.

## Note
Some like it hot. Add more or less chili powder to suit taste.

# Black Beans

| | |
|---|---|
| 1 | pound dried black beans, soaked, drained, and rinsed |
| 1 | cup chopped red onion |
| 2 | teaspoons olive oil |
| 1 | teaspoon crushed garlic |
| 1 | cup chopped celery |
| 1/2 | cup chopped bell pepper |
| 1 | can (10 ounces) Rotel diced tomatoes and chilies |
| 1 | can (14.5 ounces) diced tomatoes |
| 1/2 | teaspoon cumin |
| 1 | tablespoon chili powder |
| 2 | vegetable bouillon cubes |
| 1 | teaspoon salt |
| 1 | teaspoon ground pepper |
| 4 | cups water |
| 1 | tablespoon sugar |

1. In a large pot, sauté onion in oil over medium heat. Add garlic and sauté 1 minute.
2. Add all ingredients and cook, covered, over low heat for 3 hours. Add more water or bouillon as needed to keep mixture moist.

# POULTRY

# About Poultry

Tender and low in fat, chicken and turkey are ideal meats for healthful eating. Whether these meats are cooked with or without the skin, from a dietary perspective it is best to remove the skin before serving. I find that if chicken or turkey is to be cooked in a sauce or with a coating, it is best to remove the skin before cooking. If poultry is to be broiled or roasted alone, it is best to cook it with the skin on. The skin helps the meat retain its moisture during the cooking process, and the fat in the skin is not absorbed by the meat.

Chicken thighs are moister, tastier, and less expensive than chicken breasts. They can substitute for breasts in many of these recipes.

I often cook several pounds of chicken with salt, pepper, celery, and onion in water just to cover, being careful not to overcook. It's a great way to use "throwaway" celery leaves and outside stalks. The stock left after cooking can be used in soup or other dishes; I strain and freeze or store it, for a short time, in the refrigerator. One of my favorite ways to use the stock is to add it to the cooking water for pasta or rice.

I separate the meat itself from the skin, bones, and gristle and use it in a variety of ways—in salads, casseroles, soups, or sandwiches. It can be frozen in suitable quantities in resealable plastic bags.

Test poultry for doneness by sticking a fork in the thickest portion of the meat. If it's done, the juice will run clear, with no hint of blood.

When cooking for a crowd, keep turkey breasts in mind. They provide plenty of meat at a reasonable cost. Most recipes that call for chicken produce good results with turkey as well.

# Green Masala Chicken

**Maharaja Indian Restaurant**
*Arun Durve, Chef/Owner*

| | |
|---|---|
| 15 | mint leaves |
| 1 | cup chopped fresh cilantro |
| 5 | jalapeños, diced |
| 1 | green bell pepper, diced |
| 6 | cloves garlic |
| 2 | inches of ginger root |
| 1 | tablespoon ground cumin |
| 1 | tablespoon ground coriander |
| 2 | pounds boneless, skinless chicken breast, cut into ½-inch cubes |
| | salt to taste |
| ½ | cup canola oil |
| 1 | cup chopped onion |
| 2 | cups water |

1. Blend mint leaves, cilantro, peppers, garlic, ginger root, cumin, and coriander.
2. Put chicken pieces in a mixing bowl and add blended spices and salt. Let chicken marinate for 15 to 20 minutes.
3. Heat oil in a large pot and add onion. Sauté for 5 to 8 minutes over high heat. Add chicken and marinade and sauté for 10 minutes.
4. Add water. Cover and let cook for 15 minutes, until chicken is tender and sauce has thickened.
5. Remove to a serving dish and garnish with lemon slices and finely diced onions. Serve with basmati rice or any flatbread.

**Yield: 4 to 6 servings**

# Pan-Seared Duck Breast with Black Cherry Glaze

**Prospect Hill, The Virginia Plantation Inn**
*The Sheehan Family, Innkeepers*

| | |
|---|---|
| 3 | tablespoons olive oil |
| 2 | tablespoons finely chopped onions or shallots |
| 2 | tablespoons minced garlic |
| 3 | tablespoons balsamic vinegar |
| 1/2 | teaspoon dried thyme |
| 1/2 | cup red wine |
| 1 | cup veal or beef stock |
| 1 | pint dried black cherries |
| 2–3 | tablespoons butter |
| | salt and pepper to taste |
| | dash of sugar |
| 2 | duck breasts |
| | fresh black cherries for garnish |

1. In a saucepan, heat 2 tablespoons of the olive oil. Sauté shallots and garlic over high heat until slightly brown. Deglaze pan immediately with vinegar and add thyme.

2. Cook vinegar mixture until reduced and syrupy. Deglaze pan with red wine. Reduce liquid by one third and add stock slowly, until sauce is balanced. Add cherries and let simmer. Thicken with butter and add salt, pepper, and sugar to taste. Remove from heat.

3. Preheat cast-iron skillet until smoking. Oil pan lightly with remaining olive oil and sear duck breasts on both sides, browning them well. Lower heat and continue cooking for 3 to 6 minutes, until breasts begin to firm up. When breasts are medium rare, season with salt and pepper and remove from skillet.

4. Let rest 1 to 2 minutes. Slice breasts on the bias into 1/4-inch-thick slices (1/2 breast per person). Serve slices topped with warmed sauce and garnished with fresh cherries.

**Yield: 4 servings**

# Colonial Fried Chicken

**From the Ordinary at Michie Tavern, Circa 1784**

| | |
|---|---|
| 3/4 | cup all-purpose flour |
| 1 1/2 | tablespoons oregano |
| 1/2 | teaspoon paprika |
| 1 | teaspoon garlic salt |
| 1/4 | teaspoon pepper |
| 2–3 | pounds fryer, cut up |
| 3 | cups shortening |

1. Combine flour and seasonings. Roll chicken in flour mixture.
2. Heat shortening in a Dutch oven or other heavy, deep pan to 350 degrees.
3. Fry chicken in shortening for 12 to 15 minutes on each side, until tender.

# Grilled Lime Chicken

let stand 1 hour

| | |
|---|---|
| 1/3 | cup fresh lime juice |
| 1/2 | cup honey |
| 1/2 | cup apple juice |
| 3 | tablespoons Dijon mustard |
| 2 | tablespoons Worcestershire sauce |
| 1/2 | teaspoon salt |
| 1 | tablespoon brown sugar |
| 1 | teaspoon minced fresh basil |
| 3 | pounds chicken pieces |

1. Combine all ingredients except chicken in a saucepan and let simmer for 5 minutes.
2. Add chicken pieces and let simmer for 15 to 20 minutes.
3. Remove from heat and let stand at room temperature for about 1 hour.
4. Grill chicken pieces on a grill, browning well and basting with the marinade.

**Yield: 6 to 8 servings**

# Chicken Curry

| | |
|---|---|
| 1/2 | cup chopped onion |
| 1 | cup chopped celery |
| 1 | tablespoon olive oil |
| 1 | cup water |
| 3 | tablespoons chicken bouillon granules |
| 1 | tablespoon cornstarch |
| 1/2 | cup raisins |
| 1 | medium apple, peeled, cored, and sliced |
| 1/4 | teaspoon ground pepper |
| 3 | cups cooked, cubed chicken |
| 2–4 | teaspoons curry powder |
| 3 | cups cooked rice |
| | peanuts, chutney, raisins, and coconut to pass |

1. Sauté onion and celery in oil in a saucepan over medium heat. Add water and bouillon and bring to a boil. Turn down heat and let simmer 5 minutes.
2. Dissolve cornstarch in a little cold water. Slowly add to mixture only as much as needed to thicken slightly.
3. Add raisins, apple, pepper, and chicken. Add curry powder to taste. Simmer another 5 minutes.
4. Serve over rice. Pass dishes of peanuts, chutney, raisins, and coconut, to be added as desired.

**Note**

Don't forget the extras. Everyone loves to add his own combination.

# Easy Chicken Parmesan

| | |
|---|---|
| 2 | chicken breasts, halved, boned, and skinned |
| 1/4 | cup Italian bread crumbs |
| 3 | tablespoons grated Parmesan |
| 1 | egg |
| 1/2 | cup spaghetti or pizza sauce |
| 1/4 | teaspoon dried oregano |
| 1/2 | cup shredded mozzarella |

1. Flatten meat to 1/2-inch thickness.
2. Spray small microwave-safe baking dish with vegetable oil.
3. Combine bread crumbs and Parmesan on a plate. Beat egg in a cereal bowl. Dip cutlets in egg and coat with crumbs and cheese. Place in baking dish.
4. Pour remaining crumbs over chicken and microwave uncovered at high for 2 minutes.
5. Turn chicken over and place inner sides to the outside. Microwave at high 2 to 3 minutes more, depending on thickness.
6. Top with tomato sauce and a sprinkle of oregano. Microwave for 3 to 4 minutes more. Immediately sprinkle with mozzarella. Cover with plastic wrap and let sit for 5 minutes before serving.

**Yield: 2 to 3 servings**

# Oven-Barbecued Chicken

| | |
|---|---|
| 4 | pounds chicken pieces, cut into serving-size portions |
| 1/2 | teaspoon salt |
| 1/2 | teaspoon pepper |
| 1 | cup chopped onion |
| 1/2 | teaspoon minced garlic |
| 1 | tablespoon olive oil |
| 1/2 | cup finely chopped red pepper |
| 1/2 | cup finely chopped celery |
| 1 | cup water |
| 1 | cup catsup |
| 3 | tablespoons Worcestershire sauce |
| 2 | tablespoons cider vinegar |
| 4 | tablespoons brown sugar |
| 2 | teaspoons prepared mustard |
| 1 | teaspoon Louisiana hot sauce (optional; see note) |
| 1/4 | cup lemon juice (see note) |

1. Preheat oven to 350 degrees. Place chicken in a large baking pan in a single layer. Sprinkle with salt and pepper.
2. Bake in the oven for about 20 minutes, depending on the size of the largest pieces. Pour off any juices and fat.
3. In a large saucepan over medium heat, sauté onion and garlic in oil until golden. Add pepper and celery and cook for 2 minutes.
4. In a 1-quart measuring cup, combine the water, catsup, Worcestershire sauce, vinegar, sugar, mustard, and hot sauce. Add to the large saucepan and simmer, covered, for 30 minutes. Stir in lemon juice and remove sauce from heat.
5. Spoon one third of the sauce over the chicken. Bake for 10 minutes. Spoon half the remaining mixture over the chicken and bake another 10 minutes. Serve remaining sauce in a side dish.

**Yield: 8 to 10 servings**

**Notes**

Don't forget the lemon juice, as I have several times. It makes a big difference. The hot sauce makes for a very hot sauce.

# Creamed Chicken with Peas

| | |
|---|---|
| 4 | tablespoons butter |
| 4 | tablespoons flour |
| 2 | cups milk |
| 2 | cups cooked, cubed chicken |
| 4 | tablespoons finely chopped onion |
| 2 | tablespoons chopped parsley |
| 1/2 | teaspoon salt |
| 1/4 | teaspoon ground pepper |
| 1 | cup peas, fresh or frozen |
| 4 | slices toast or biscuits |

1. In a microwavable bowl, cook butter and flour at high for 1 minute. Slowly add milk and whisk briskly. Microwave 2 to 3 minutes more, whisking after each minute.
2. Add remaining ingredients except toast. Stir well and microwave at medium for 6 minutes. Stir well and serve over toast, toast cups (see note), or biscuits.

**Note**

To make toast cups, cut the crust off slices of soft bread. Butter custard cups or the cups of a muffin tin. Mold the bread into the cups and bake in a 350-degree oven for 5 minutes.

**Variation**

This can be served as a pot pie by making a topping from frozen puff pastry. See page 165.

# Chicken Pot Pie

| | |
|---|---|
| 10 | ounces frozen peas and carrots |
| 1/2 | cup water |
| 4 | tablespoons butter |
| 1/2 | cup chopped onion |
| 1/2 | cup chopped mushrooms |
| 1/3 | cup flour |
| 1/2 | teaspoon salt |
| 1/2 | teaspoon dried thyme |
| 1/4 | teaspoon ground pepper |
| 2 | cups chicken broth |
| 3/4 | cup milk |
| 3 | cups cubed, cooked chicken |
| 1/4 | cup chopped fresh parsley |
| 1/2 | package frozen puff pastry, thawed |

1. Preheat oven to 400 degrees. Cook peas and carrots in a saucepan with 1/2 cup of water until just tender. Drain.
2. In a large saucepan, heat butter and add onion and mushrooms. Cook over medium heat until tender. Stir in flour, salt, thyme, and pepper. Add broth and milk and whisk until smooth and thickened.
3. Stir in peas and carrots, chicken, and parsley.
4. Cut the puff pastry to the shape of the casserole you are going to use (see note). Add 1 inch for shrinkage. Transfer to an ungreased cookie sheet, prick all over with a fork, and bake for about 10 minutes.
5. Pour the chicken mixture into casserole and top with the baked crust. Turn oven down to 300 degrees and keep casserole hot until ready to serve.

## Note

For a nice presentation, cut the puff pastry in circles or fancy shapes to top individual bowls.

## Variation

Chicken Pot Pie can be topped with any flattened, refrigerated dough rather than baked pastry and baked at 400 degrees for about 15 minutes.

# Chicken Stir-Fry

| | |
|---|---|
| ¼ | cup chopped celery |
| ¼ | cup chopped green pepper |
| 1 | teaspoon olive oil |
| 8 | ounces pineapple chunks with juice |
| 2 | cups cubed cooked chicken (see note) |
| ½ | tablespoon cornstarch |
| ½ | cup chicken broth |
| 1½ | teaspoons soy sauce |
| 2 | tablespoons sugar |
| 1 | tablespoon vinegar |

1. In a skillet or wok, sauté celery and green pepper in oil for a few minutes, until just softened. Add pineapple and chicken.
2. In a small cup, combine cornstarch and broth. Stir into the skillet. Add soy sauce, sugar, and vinegar and stir well until thickened slightly. Serve on rice or noodles.

**Note**

You may also start with uncooked chicken. First, sauté the chicken cubes in olive oil over medium-high heat for 7 to 10 minutes, until well done. Then proceed as directed.

# Chicken Almondine

| | |
|---|---|
| 3 | cups cubed cooked chicken |
| 10 | ounces cream of chicken condensed soup |
| 8 | ounces sliced water chestnuts |
| $^2/_3$ | cup Miracle Whip |
| $^1/_2$ | cup sour cream or yogurt |
| $^1/_2$ | cup chopped celery |
| $^1/_2$ | cup chopped onion |
| 8 | ounces Pillsbury Crescent rolls |
| $^1/_2$ | cup shredded Swiss cheese |
| 2 | ounces slivered almonds |

1. Preheat oven to 375 degrees.
2. In a large saucepan, combine chicken, soup, water chestnuts, Miracle Whip, sour cream or yogurt, celery, and onion. Heat slowly over low heat, stirring gently, until almost boiling.
3. Pour into an ungreased, 12 x 8-inch baking dish.
4. Unfold rolls into two flat pieces of dough and cover casserole. Sprinkle with Swiss cheese and almonds and cover with aluminum foil.
5. Bake for 30 to 40 minutes. Remove foil and bake another 10 minutes. Serve.

**Yield: 4 to 6 servings**

**Note**
This may be frozen and reheated, but it is best served soon after preparing.

**Variation**
Add 1 cup frozen peas.

# Cashew Chicken

| | |
|---|---|
| 1 | tablespoon olive oil |
| 3–4 | cups diced chicken breast, skinned and trimmed of fat |
| 1/2 | cup chopped onion |
| 1/2 | cup diced green pepper |
| 1/2 | pound mushrooms, sliced |
| 1/4 | cup soy sauce |
| 1 | teaspoon sugar |
| 1 | tablespoon cornstarch |
| 1 | cup chicken broth |
| 3/4 | cup cashew pieces |
| 2 | cups cooked rice or noodles |

1. In a frying pan, heat oil and brown chicken on all sides over medium-high heat.
2. Add onion, pepper, and mushrooms and stir-fry about 2 minutes.
3. Combine soy, sugar, cornstarch, and broth in a small bowl.
4. Whisk into chicken mixture. Turn down heat and let simmer 10 to 15 minutes.
5. Add cashews. Stir and serve over rice or noodles.

**Yield: 3 to 4 servings**

**Variations**
Turkey or pork will work just as well as chicken.

# Lemon Chicken

| | |
|---|---|
| 4 | serving-size pieces of boneless chicken breast |
| 1/4 | teaspoon salt |
| 1/4 | teaspoon coarsely ground fresh black pepper |
| 2 | tablespoons olive oil or butter |
| 1/4 | cup chopped fresh parsley |
| 1/4 | cup chopped fresh chives or green onions |
| 1/4 | cup lemon juice |
| 1/2 | cup chicken broth |
| 3 | tablespoons brandy (optional) |

1. Pound breast to 1-inch thickness and season with salt and pepper.
2. Heat oil or butter in a small skillet. Over medium-high heat, sauté breasts for 4 minutes on each side or until cooked through.
3. Remove chicken to a platter. Add parsley and chives or green onions to the skillet and sauté 1 minute. Add lemon juice, broth, and brandy. Whisk and simmer for 1 to 2 minutes. Pour over chicken and serve.

# Crunchy Lemon Chicken

| | |
|---|---|
| 1 1/2 | cups bran flakes, crushed |
| 1/4 | teaspoon salt |
| 1/2 | teaspoon grated lemon peel |
| 1 | egg white |
| 1 | teaspoon lemon juice |
| 1 | pound chicken breasts, boned, skinned, and quartered |

1. Preheat oven to 350 degrees.
2. Combine bran flakes, salt, and lemon peel in a shallow bowl.
3. Combine egg white and lemon juice and beat.
4. Dip chicken pieces in egg white, then coat well with bran flake mixture.
5. Place pieces in an 8 x 8-inch baking pan that has been sprayed with vegetable oil. Bake 20 to 30 minutes.

**Variation**
Substitute lime juice for the lemon juice for a slightly different flavor.

# Kathy's Marinated Chicken Breasts

**marinate overnight**

| | |
|---|---|
| 1/2 | cup apricot preserves |
| 1 | cup orange marmalade |
| 1 | package Lipton dry onion soup mix |
| 1/2 | cup Southern Comfort |
| 1/4 | cup orange juice |
| 4 | chicken breasts, halved, boned, and skinned |

1. Combine all ingredients except chicken in a saucepan and simmer for 3 to 5 minutes, until just well blended.
2. If chicken breast halves are large, halve them again. Place in a plastic or glass flat pan and pour hot marinade over. Let cool and refrigerate, covered, overnight or all day. Once cool, chicken and marinade may be placed in a plastic resealable bag for refrigeration.
3. Bake chicken in the marinade at 350 degrees for 35 to 40 minutes, basting occasionally.

**Yield: 6 to 8 servings**


# Barbecued Chicken Breasts

| | |
|---|---|
| 1/3 | cup catsup |
| 2 | teaspoons lime or lemon juice |
| 1/4 | teaspoon crushed garlic |
| 1/8 | teaspoon ground pepper |
| 1 | teaspoon hot pepper sauce |
| 2 | tablespoons sugar |
| 1 | teaspoon Worcestershire sauce |
| 4 | chicken breast halves, boned and skinned |

1. Combine all ingredients but chicken in a bowl. Add chicken and marinate in the refrigerator for as long as time permits, up to 4 hours.
2. Grill or broil chicken pieces, basting often with the marinade.
3. Bring remaining marinade to a boil and serve as a sauce with the chicken.

# Skinny-Dip Chicken

| | |
|---|---|
| ¹/₂ | teaspoon ground pepper |
| ¹/₄ | teaspoon garlic powder |
| ¹/₂ | teaspoon salt |
| 1 | teaspoon crushed oregano |
| ¹/₂ | teaspoon paprika |
| ²/₃ | cup flour |
| 4 | cups corn flakes, crushed |
| 2–3 | pounds chicken, skinned and cut in pieces |
| 1 | cup milk |

1. Preheat oven to 400 degrees.
2. Combine spices and flour in a shallow bowl. Place corn flakes in a flat dish.
3. Dip chicken pieces in milk and then in flour mixture, turning to coat.
4. Dip chicken pieces in milk again, then roll in corn flakes until coated.
5. Place a rack in a roasting pan and lay chicken on the rack. Spray the top of the chicken with vegetable oil.
6. Bake for 35 minutes or until juices run clear.

# Yogurt Chicken

| | |
|---|---|
| 1 | cup plain yogurt |
| 2 | teaspoons curry powder |
| ¹/₂ | teaspoon salt |
| 1¹/₂ | teaspoons ground pepper |
| 1 | teaspoon paprika |
| 2 | small chicken breasts, bone in but skinned and trimmed of fat |
| 1 | cup bread crumbs |

1. Preheat oven to 350 degrees.
2. In a small, shallow bowl, combine yogurt with curry, salt, pepper, and paprika.
3. Dip each breast in the yogurt mixture and then coat with bread crumbs. Place in a shallow 8 x 8-inch baking pan.
4. Bake for about 40 minutes, depending upon the thickness of the breasts.

# Chicken Florentine

| | |
|---|---|
| 1 | pound chicken breasts, skinned, boned, and quartered |
| 3/4 | cup chicken broth |
| 3 | tablespoons white wine |
| 1 | pound fresh spinach |
| 2 | tablespoons cornstarch |
| 3 | ounces cream cheese |
| 1 | tablespoon lemon juice |
| 1 | tablespoon butter |
| 2 | cups cooked rice |

1. In a small pan, poach chicken in broth and white wine for 10 to 12 minutes, until done. Remove from pan and slice into 1-inch strips.
2. Stem, wash, and steam spinach until just tender.
3. Add cornstarch to broth in pan. Stir in cream cheese.
4. Toss spinach with lemon juice and butter.
5. Mound rice in the center of each plate and encircle with spinach. Place chicken on top of rice and top with sauce.

**Yield: 4 servings**

During the American Revolution, four thousand British and Hessian prisoners of war were held at Col. John Harvie's Charlottesville farm. They soon laid out a small town that included a theater, a coffeehouse, and a cold bath. The quarters were called The Barracks, and the name is preserved today in Barracks Road.

# Chicken with Raspberry Vinegar

| | |
|---|---|
| 2 | tablespoons olive oil |
| 1 | cup finely chopped onion |
| 1 | teaspoon crushed garlic |
| 1¼ | pounds chicken breasts, skinned and boned |
| 2 | tablespoons raspberry vinegar |
| 2 | tablespoons balsamic vinegar |
| 1 | teaspoon Dijon mustard |
| ¼ | cup chopped fresh basil |
| 1 | teaspoon chopped fresh rosemary |
| 1 | teaspoon chopped fresh oregano |
| ¼ | teaspoon ginger |
| | salt and pepper to taste (optional) |

1. Heat oil in a skillet over medium-high heat. Add onions and garlic and sauté until just tender.
2. Cut chicken into 1-inch pieces and add to skillet. Cook until browned, about 3 minutes. Reduce heat.
3. Stir in vinegars and mustard. Add seasonings and cook until chicken is tender and cooked through, stirring constantly. Add salt and pepper if desired.

# Grilled Chicken with Artichoke Salsa

| | |
|---|---|
| 1 | jar (6 ounces) marinated artichoke hearts |
| ½ | cup medium tomato salsa |
| 1 | pound chicken breast pieces, skinned, boned, and trimmed of fat |

1. Drain artichokes and reserve juice. In a food processor, blend artichokes and salsa.
2. Flatten chicken breast pieces to ½-inch thickness.
3. Place chicken in a resealable plastic bag with the artichoke marinade. Refrigerate until ready to cook, at least 30 minutes.
4. Grill or broil chicken until browned and cooked through.
5. In a pan, bring salsa to a boil. Pour over chicken and serve.

# Chicken with Orange

  2 pounds chicken breasts, skinned, boned, and cut into serving pieces
 12 ounces frozen orange juice concentrate, thawed
  1 envelope Lipton dry onion soup mix
 11 ounces mandarin oranges, drained

1. Preheat oven to 350 degrees.
2. Place chicken in a shallow baking dish. Combine orange juice and onion mix and pour over chicken.
3. Bake for 40 minutes.
4. Pour mandarin oranges over chicken and return to oven for another 10 minutes.

**Note**
Leftovers may be frozen or refrigerated for the next day.


# Chicken Thighs with Dressing

This requires very little preparation time and is a whole meal with a salad or vegetable. The recipe is also easily doubled or halved.

  6 ounces Stove Top dressing
5–8 chicken thighs, skinned and fat removed
  1/2 teaspoon salt
  1/4 teaspoon pepper

1. Preheat oven to 375 degrees.
2. Prepare Stove Top dressing according to directions. Place in a shallow baking dish and pat down flat.
3. Top with chicken thighs. Sprinkle with salt and pepper.
4. Cover with foil and bake in oven for 50 minutes. Uncover and bake about 10 minutes more. To check for doneness, cut and see if the juices run clear.

**Yield: 3 to 4 servings**

# Easy Chicken

4   pieces chicken, bone in but skinned

4   ounces Italian dressing

1. Preheat oven to 350 degrees.
2. Place chicken in a greased baking dish and pour dressing over. Cover with foil and bake for 20 minutes.
3. Remove foil, turn chicken over, and bake uncovered for another 15 minutes, until well done.

**Variation**

Substitute French for Italian dressing and sprinkle chicken with some grated Parmesan after turning over.

# Chicken Fried Rice

1/2   cup chopped onion

1/4   cup chopped green pepper

1/4   cup chopped celery

1   tablespoon olive oil

1   cup cubed or shredded cooked chicken

1   tablespoon soy sauce plus additional to taste

2 1/2   cups chicken broth

1   cup uncooked long-grain white rice

2   eggs, slightly beaten (optional)

    salt and pepper to taste

1. In a large skillet with a cover, sauté onion, pepper, and celery in oil over medium heat until translucent.
2. Add chicken, soy sauce, broth, and rice. Turn heat down to a simmer and cover. Simmer 20 minutes, until rice is tender.
3. Remove cover. Turn up heat and reduce any liquid remaining in the skillet, stirring well to avoid burning chicken and rice. Stir in egg and cook for 1 minute.
4. Season with salt and pepper or more soy sauce and serve.

# Turkey Turnovers

| | |
|---|---|
| 1/2 | cup finely chopped onion |
| 1/2 | teaspoon crushed garlic |
| 1 | tablespoon olive oil |
| 1 | tablespoon butter |
| 1 | cup frozen peas and carrots, thawed |
| 1 | tablespoon flour |
| 1/3 | cup heavy cream |
| 1 1/2 | cups chopped cooked turkey |
| 1/2 | teaspoon dried thyme |
| 1/4 | teaspoon salt |
| 1/4 | teaspoon pepper |
| 1 | package (17 1/4 ounces) frozen puff pastry, thawed |

1. Preheat oven to 400 degrees.
2. In a skillet, sauté onion and garlic in olive oil and butter until translucent.
3. Add peas and carrots and turn down heat. Simmer until just tender, stirring often.
4. Add flour and cook for 1 minute. Stir in cream and simmer until thickened.
5. Add turkey, thyme, salt, and pepper. Simmer until fairly thick. Remove from heat.
6. Unfold pastry sheets and cut each into 4 squares. Spoon the turkey mixture into the center of each square. Brush edges with water and fold in half to form triangles. Press edges with a fork to seal.
7. Place on an ungreased cookie sheet and bake for 15 minutes, until golden brown.

**Note**

Turkey Turnovers freeze well.

# Chicken Enchiladas

|   4   | cups mild or medium-hot salsa |
|-------|-------------------------------|
|   1   | pound chicken breast, skinned, boned, and cut into bite-size pieces |
| 3/4   | cup vegetable oil |
| 12–18 | 6-inch corn tortillas |
|   3   | cups shredded Monterey Jack |
|   1   | cup finely sliced lettuce |
|   1   | tomato, chopped |
| 1/2   | cup sour cream |
|   1   | avocado, sliced (optional) |

1. In a small saucepan, heat 2 cups of the salsa. Add chicken and cook over medium heat for 15 to 20 minutes.
2. Spread 1/2 cup of the remaining salsa in the bottom of a baking pan.
3. In a small frying pan, heat oil until hot but not smoking. Lay out paper towels three-deep on the counter. Using tongs, dip each tortilla in the hot oil for about 30 seconds. Blot off the excess oil on the paper towels.
4. Put a heaping tablespoon of chicken and salsa in the middle of each tortilla. Add a full teaspoon of cheese and roll up. Place in the baking pan. Repeat until all tortillas are in the baking pan.
5. Spread 1–1 1/2 cups of remaining salsa over the tortillas and top with 1 cup of cheese.
6. Refrigerate until ready to bake, 20 to 30 minutes at 350 degrees.
7. Serve with lettuce, tomato, sour cream, salsa, avocado, and remaining cheese on the side.

**Yield: about 4 servings**

# Chicken Tortillas with Feta

| | |
|---|---|
| 4 | 8-inch flour tortillas |
| 2/3 | cup thinly sliced tomatoes |
| 2 | green onions, thinly sliced |
| 1 1/2 | cups shredded cooked chicken |
| 1/3 | cup mild or medium tomato salsa |
| 2 | ounces feta |
| 1 | teaspoon dried crushed basil |
| 2 | tablespoons sliced ripe olives |

1. Preheat oven to 350 degrees.
2. Bake tortillas on an oiled cookie sheet about 7 minutes, until crisp, turning once.
3. Top each tortilla with tomatoes, onions, and chicken. Spoon salsa over each and sprinkle with feta, basil, and olives.
4. Bake in the oven for 7 to 12 minutes more, until cheese is melted and ingredients are heated through.

# SEAFOOD

About Fish
Cooper's Crab Cakes
Fall Orchard Tuna
Roasted Garlic Polenta with Whole Shrimp
and Fresh Asparagus
Pan-Seared Grouper with Tomato-Garlic Crust
in Sauce Provençal
Broiled Fillet
Chesapeake Bay Flounder
Sole in White Wine
Flounder Fillets with Sesame Seeds
Baked Fillets with Lemon Stuffing
Halibut with Roasted Red Pepper Sauce
Fish Florentine
Virginia Crab Cakes
Fettuccine with Crab
Shrimp or Scallop Stir-Fry
Crab Imperial
Sautéed Shrimp
Shrimp Creole
Shrimp or Lobster Newburg
Grilled Swordfish with Sherry Sauce
Marinated Salmon
Salmon Steak with Cream Sauce
Skillet Salmon with Curry
Baked Salmon with Almonds
Shrimp Tacos
Baked Clams

# About Fish

Today, we can try fish from all over the world. The variety is nothing short of wonderful. Mahi mahi and orange roughy, which are similar to haddock, are now in our markets, and fish like shark and tilapia are also more readily available than they once were. Shark is comparable to swordfish and tilapia to flounder, and both are worth trying.

Nor should the merits of less exotic fish be overlooked. Fresh bluefish and tuna, for example, are often shunned because of their strong flavor. They do have more fish oil than some other fish (which means they are better for you), so bluefish and tuna fillets that are not really fresh do have a fishy taste. But no fish is better than a bluefish fresh from the ocean.

Generally, if fish smells fishy, it isn't good. Fish no more than a day old is best. If that isn't an option, it's been my experience that flash-frozen fish is preferable to fish thawed at the store for a day or two. Ask the seller for frozen, rather than already thawed, fish. It is best to use fish the day you buy it, but you can keep it frozen for up to a month. Just before cooking, thaw it in the microwave or in cool water. Never leave fish in the refrigerator for more than a few hours; it isn't cold enough there to keep the oils from spoiling.

Fish can be broiled, poached, baked, fried, microwaved, or grilled. Each method has its advantages. Just be careful; seafood takes very little time to cook, and over-cooked fish is dry and tasteless. For fillets, the rule of thumb is 10 minutes for each inch of thickness, unless cooked in a sauce. For fish cooked in a sauce, 15 minutes per inch will be about right. Fillets more than an inch thick need to be turned when broiling or grilling. When the fish is done, it will flake easily with a fork. Shrimp and scallops become opaque when cooked through.

I keep a bag of flash-frozen flounder fillets in my freezer for days when I'm in a hurry or don't want a lot of bother. If I get home in time, I bake several potatoes in the oven for about 40 minutes at 400 degrees. I put some lettuce and tomato on a plate and some broccoli or frozen peas in a pan on the stove. When the potatoes are done I remove them from the oven, turn on the heat under the vegetable, and turn the oven to broil. In goes a piece of flounder coated with 1 teaspoon of mayonnaise and sprinkled with Parmesan. In about 3 minutes I test the fish with a fork to see if it is flaky and done. Supper is ready, and I have spent about 8 minutes in the kitchen. I also have an extra potato or two cooked for another meal.

# Cooper's Crab Cakes

**The Edge at Cooper's Vantage Restaurant, Wintergreen Resort**
*David Hayden, Chef*

| | |
|---|---|
| 1 | cup mayonnaise |
| 2 | tablespoons yellow mustard |
| 2 | tablespoons Grey Poupon |
| 1/2 | cup minced celery |
| 1/2 | large red bell pepper, minced |
| 1 | egg |
| 2 | tablespoons Worcestershire sauce |
| 2 | tablespoons Tabasco |
| 1/2 | teaspoon lemon juice |
| 1 | tablespoon Old Bay seasoning |
| 2 | tablespoons plain bread crumbs |
| 20 | ounces fresh backfin crabmeat, picked of cartilage |

1. Preheat oven to 425 degrees.
2. In a bowl, combine all ingredients except crabmeat. Mix well to form sauce.
3. Add sauce to crabmeat a little at a time, until a firm but rich consistency is achieved. Form into 3-ounce cakes.
4. Bake in oven for 10 to 12 minutes. Crab cakes should be golden brown with a light crust.

# Fall Orchard Tuna

**Devils Grill Restaurant, Wintergreen Resort**
*Aaron Fultz, Chef*

| | |
|---|---|
| 3 | medium Red Bliss potatoes, thinly sliced |
| 1 | teaspoon dried rosemary |
| 3 | tablespoons olive oil |
| 1/4 | Granny Smith apple, thinly julienned |
| 1/4 | Red Delicious apple, thinly julienned |
| 1/2 | fresh peach, peeled and thinly julienned |
| 3 | 1/2-inch slices of Spanish onion |
| 2 | ounces (4 tablespoons) butter, melted |
| 1/2 | teaspoon tarragon |
| 8 | ounces yellowfin tuna fillet |
| 1 | teaspoon cracked black pepper |

1. Preheat oven to 350 degrees.
2. Coat potatoes with rosemary and 2 tablespoons of the olive oil and bake in the oven until done, about 15 minutes.
3. Toss apples, peach, and onion with butter and tarragon in a baking dish. Increase the oven temperature to 375 degrees and bake until fruit is tender and onions caramelize (turn a deep brown), about 20 minutes.
4. Rub tuna fillet with remaining olive oil and cracked black pepper. Chargrill to desired temperature and serve with warm fruit sauce and potatoes.

# Roasted Garlic Polenta with Whole Shrimp and Fresh Asparagus

**Sweetbones**
*Peter A. Murphy, Chef and Owner*

| | |
|---|---|
| 3 | tablespoons butter |
| 2 | tablespoons chopped fresh garlic |
| 2 | tablespoons chopped fresh shallots |
| 2 | cups chicken or vegetable stock |
| 1 | cup water |
| 1 | pound large, raw shrimp, peeled |
| 1/2 | pound fresh asparagus, cut in 2-inch pieces |
| 1 | cup yellow cornmeal |

1. In a large saucepan, melt butter and sauté garlic and shallots until translucent.
2. Add stock and water and bring to a rolling boil. Add shrimp and asparagus and return to a rolling boil.
3. Whisking constantly, slowly add cornmeal to boiling liquid until mixture begins to pull away from the sides of the pan.
4. Spread mixture in a nonstick, 9 x 12-inch baking pan. Let cool and slice into squares.
5. Grill or serve as is.

# Pan-Seared Grouper with Tomato-Garlic Crust in Sauce Provençal

**Tastings of Charlottesville**
*Bill Curtis, Owner/Chef*

| | |
|---|---|
| 2 | 6-ounce boneless, skinless grouper fillets |
| 1 | clove garlic, pureed |
| | tomato powder for dusting (see note) |
| 4 | shallots, finely chopped |
| 1 | medium bulb of fennel, finely chopped |
| | pinch of chopped fennel seeds |
| 1 | teaspoon chopped garlic |
| | olive oil for sautéing |
| 4 | Roma tomatoes, coarsely chopped |
| 1 | quart fish fumet |
| 1 | cup dry, aromatic white wine (e.g., sauvignon blanc) |
| 2 | sweet red peppers, steamed, peeled, and pureed |
| | lemon juice or rice wine vinegar to taste |
| | sea salt to taste |
| 2 | heaping teaspoons roux (approximate) |
| | lemon stars for garnish |

1. Preheat oven to 350 degrees.
2. Rub grouper with pureed garlic and dust with tomato powder. Set aside.
3. In a large saucepan, sauté shallots, chopped fennel bulb and seeds, and garlic in oil for about 5 minutes, until slightly underdone. Add tomatoes to pan and heat through.
4. Add fumet and wine to pan and bring to a boil. Let simmer for 15 minutes.
5. Add red peppers to slightly reduced sauce and let simmer for 5 minutes. Add lemon juice and sea salt. Thicken slightly with roux and remove from heat.
6. Heat olive oil in a frying pan until just smoking. Add fillets and turn almost immediately. (If you want a blackened feel to the fish, don't turn right away.) Set skillet in the oven for 16 to 20 minutes (8 to 10 minutes for a convection oven), depending on the thickness of the fish, until fish is cooked to an internal temperature of 130 to 140 degrees.

7.  Pour Provençal sauce on a plate. Place fish on top and garnish with lemon stars. Serve with a seafood-flavored rice pilaf or garlic mashed potatoes.

**Note**

Tomato powder is an ingredient used by pasta makers and available only in specialty stores.

# Broiled Fillet

- 1   **pound fish fillet**
- 1   **teaspoon Old Bay seasoning (approximate)**
- 2   **tablespoons lemon juice or white wine (approximate)**
- 1   **teaspoon butter (optional)**

1.  Place a piece of aluminum foil in a baking pan and spray with vegetable oil. Place fish on foil in a single layer and sprinkle with seasoning and lemon juice or wine. Place a lump of butter on each piece if desired.
2.  Broil about 3 inches from heat for 3 to 8 minutes, depending on the thickness of the fillets. Test with a fork.

**Notes**

This recipe's ingredient amounts are easily varied. Figure about 1 teaspoon Old Bay seasoning and 2 tablespoons lemon juice or wine per pound of fish.

Don't buy cooking wines. If a wine isn't good enough to drink, it isn't good enough for cooking. This is especially important when the delicate flavor of fish comes into play.

# Chesapeake Bay Flounder

| | |
|---|---|
| 1½ | pounds small flounder fillets |
| 4 | tablespoons dry cereal crumbs or bread crumbs |
| 1 | tablespoon butter |
| | salt and pepper to taste |
| ¾ | cup milk |

1. Preheat oven to 350 degrees.
2. Spray a foil-lined, 8 x 8-inch pan with vegetable oil.
3. Place fillets on foil and sprinkle with crumbs. Dot with butter and dust with salt and pepper. Gently pour milk over all.
4. Bake for 10 to 20 minutes, until fish flakes easily. Brown briefly under the broiler if desired.

In March 1853, long before he became the Confederate raider known as the Grey Ghost, John Singleton Mosby interrupted his studies as a third-year UVa student by shooting the son of a local tavern keeper. He was fined five hundred dollars and sentenced to a year in prison. During his prison stay, he studied law by borrowing books from the attorney who prosecuted his case. Two years later he was admitted to the Albemarle County bar.

# Sole in White Wine

marinate 2 hours

June Harris of Charlottesville won a prize in the Lawry's Cook-Off with this recipe.

| | |
|---|---|
| 4 | fillets of sole or other mild white fish |
| 1/2 | teaspoon Lawry's seasoned salt |
| 1/2 | teaspoon Lawry's lemon pepper marinade |
| 1 | cup dry white wine |
| 1 | whole shallot, chopped |
| 1/4 | cup butter |
| 2 | egg yolks |
| 1/4 | cup cashews (optional) |

1. Place fillets in a shallow dish and sprinkle with seasoned salt and marinade. Add wine and refrigerate for 2 hours.
2. Drain fillets and set aside, reserving marinade.
3. In a skillet over low heat, sauté shallot in butter until lightly browned. Add fillets and cook for 2 to 3 minutes, until just flaky. Remove.
4. Add all but 1/4 cup of the marinade to the skillet.
5. Whisk egg yolks into the remaining 1/4 cup marinade. Stir into skillet mixture.
6. Cook, stirring constantly, over low heat until thickened. Return fillets to the sauce and heat thoroughly.
7. Remove to plates or a platter and sprinkle with cashews if desired.

**Yield: 4 servings**

**Note**
This is especially nice served with rice and broccoli.

# Flounder Fillets with Sesame Seeds

1/2    **teaspoon finely chopped garlic**

1/2    **cup diced ripe tomato**

1    **teaspoon chopped fresh basil or 1/3 teaspoon dried basil**

1/2    **teaspoon sugar**

1    **tablespoon olive oil**

2    **tablespoons sesame seeds**

1/2    **pound flounder fillet**

1/2    **teaspoon salt**

1/8    **teaspoon ground pepper**

    **lemon wedges for garnish**

1. In a 1-pint measuring cup, combine garlic, tomato, basil, sugar, and 1 teaspoon of the oil. Microwave at high for 2 minutes. Stir. Microwave for 1 minute more.
2. Spread sesame seeds on a flat plate. Season fillet with salt and pepper and lay on plate to coat with seeds. Turn over to coat both sides.
3. Heat remaining 2 teaspoons of the oil in a nonstick frying pan. Add fillet and cook over medium heat, turning as needed, until fillet is golden brown on each side. Cooking time will depend on the thickness of the fillet (approximately 10 minutes per inch of thickness).
4. Place fillet on a warm plate and top with tomato mixture. Serve with a lemon wedge.

# Baked Fillets with Lemon Stuffing

| | |
|---|---|
| 1/2 | cup chopped onion |
| 1/2 | cup chopped celery |
| 4 | tablespoons butter |
| 4 | cups bread crumbs or finely broken bread |
| 1/2 | teaspoon salt |
| 1/2 | teaspoon ground pepper |
| 1 | teaspoon grated lemon rind |
| 1/4 | cup water |
| 1/4 | cup lemon juice |
| 2 | pounds mild white fish fillets |
| 1 | lemon, thinly sliced |

1. Preheat oven to 350 degrees.
2. In a skillet, sauté onion and celery in 3 tablespoons of the butter until just crisp-tender. Remove from heat and add bread crumbs, salt, pepper, lemon rind, water, and lemon juice.
3. Spread stuffing in the bottom of a greased casserole. Place fish on top. Place lemon slices on the fish and dot with remaining butter.
4. Bake uncovered for 20 to 30 minutes, until fish flakes.

**Yield: 4 to 6 servings**

**Variation**

Use Stove Top dressing for a quick and easy meal. Add the lemon rind and juice to flavor it.

# Halibut with Roasted Red Pepper Sauce

²/₃   cup roasted red peppers

2   tablespoons heavy cream

¹/₈   teaspoon salt

¹/₈   teaspoon ground pepper

1   tablespoon butter, melted

1   tablespoon fresh lemon juice

1   pound halibut steak

     chopped parsley for garnish

1.  In a blender, process red peppers until pureed.
2.  Transfer to a saucepan and add cream, salt, and pepper. Bring mixture to a boil, adding a bit of water if necessary for a good consistency. Let simmer over low heat for a few minutes.
3.  Combine butter and lemon juice.
4.  Broil halibut about 4 inches from heat, basting with butter mixture, for 7 to 10 minutes. Turn once if steak is one inch or more in thickness.
5.  Pour sauce onto a heated platter and place halibut on top. Decorate with parsley.

**Note**

The sauce is a great one for all kinds of fish.

# Fish Florentine

| | |
|---|---|
| 1 | pound flounder or other mild fish fillet |
| 1/4 | teaspoon salt |
| 1/4 | teaspoon ground pepper |
| 1/4 | teaspoon tarragon |
| 2 | tablespoons lemon juice |
| 1 | package frozen chopped spinach, thawed |
| 1 | egg, beaten |
| 2 | tablespoons butter |
| 2 | tablespoons chopped onion |
| 2 | teaspoons cornstarch |
| 1/2 | cup milk |
| 1/4 | cup white wine |
| 1/2 | cup grated Cheddar |

1. Preheat oven to 350 degrees.
2. Pat fish dry and season with salt, pepper, tarragon, and lemon juice. Set aside.
3. Drain spinach well and combine with egg. Place in the bottom of an 8 x 8-inch baking pan.
4. In a saucepan over medium heat, simmer butter and onion.
5. Mix cornstarch into a little milk, then add all the milk and cornstarch to saucepan. Stir well until mixture thickens. Add wine. Do not boil.
6. Place fillets on spinach and top with sauce.
7. Sprinkle cheese over all and bake for 30 minutes, until fish is done.

# Virginia Crab Cakes

| | |
|---|---|
| ¼ | cup chopped onion |
| 2 | tablespoons butter |
| 3 | eggs |
| ⅔ | cup fine bread crumbs plus additional for dredging |
| 2 | teaspoons Worcestershire sauce |
| 1 | teaspoon Old Bay seasoning |
| 1 | teaspoon dry mustard |
| 12 | ounces canned crabmeat, drained and cartilage removed |
| ¼ | cup vegetable oil |

1. In a small saucepan, sauté onion in butter until tender.
2. In a mixing bowl, beat eggs and add bread crumbs, Worcestershire, Old Bay, and mustard. Mix well.
3. Stir in flaked crabmeat and onion mixture.
4. Form into six ½-inch-thick patties. Dust with extra bread crumbs.
5. In a heavy skillet, heat oil until hot but not smoking. Fry the patties, three at a time, in the hot fat, turning once. Drain on paper towels.

**Note**

If you love crab cakes but haven't the crab, try the Mock Crab Cakes on page 213. Some Eastern Shore residents say they can't tell the difference.

# Fettuccine with Crab

Served with a salad, this is a full, simple meal that's suitable for company.

| | |
|---|---|
| 8 | ounces fettuccine |
| 1½ | cups whipping cream |
| 6 | ounces crabmeat, cartilage removed |
| ¾ | cup grated Parmesan |
| ¼ | teaspoon salt |
| ¼ | teaspoon ground pepper |
| ¼ | cup chopped parsley |

1. Cook pasta according to package directions until al dente. Drain.
2. In a large skillet over medium-low heat, bring cream just to a boil. Cook slowly for 1 to 3 minutes, until reduced and slightly thickened.
3. Stir in crabmeat, ½ cup of the Parmesan, salt, pepper, and parsley. Heat through for about 5 minutes.
4. Toss sauce with pasta, sprinkle with remaining cheese, and serve.

**Yield: 4 servings**

# Shrimp or Scallop Stir-Fry

$^1/_2$     cup water

1     tablespoon cornstarch

2     tablespoons soy sauce

$^1/_8$     teaspoon ground ginger

1     teaspoon chicken bouillon granules

1     tablespoon olive oil

$^1/_2$     teaspoon minced garlic

$^1/_2$     cup onion quarters

$^1/_2$     cup sliced bell pepper

$^1/_2$     jalepeño, finely diced (optional)

$^2/_3$     cup fresh pea pods

8     ounces shrimp, rinsed, peeled, and deveined, or 8 ounces scallops, rinsed

4     ounces water chestnuts

$1^1/_2$     cups cooked rice or noodles

1. In a small bowl, combine water, cornstarch, soy sauce, ginger, and bouillon.
2. Preheat a skillet or wok at high temperature and add 2 teaspoons of the oil.
3. Sauté garlic, onion, peppers, and pea pods over medium heat for about 2 minutes, until crisp-tender. Remove to a dish.
4. Turn heat down just a bit, add remaining teaspoon of oil, and stir-fry shrimp or scallops until opaque, about 3 minutes.
5. Pour water mixture into center of the skillet and stir vigorously until thickened and clear.
6. Add water chestnuts and vegetables and stir until everything is hot and coated with sauce.
7. Serve over warm rice or noodles.

**Yield: 2 servings**

**Note**

Refrigerated leftovers will be good the next day, but I don't recommend freezing.

# Crab Imperial

| | |
|---|---|
| 1 | tablespoon chopped green pepper |
| 1 | teaspoon butter |
| 2 | tablespoons all-purpose flour |
| 1 | tablespoon pimento |
| 1 | tablespoon mustard |
| 1/3 | cup heavy cream |
| 1/3 | cup mayonnaise |
| 1 | tablespoon sherry |
| 1 | pound crabmeat, cartilage removed |

1. Preheat oven to 350 degrees.
2. In a skillet over medium heat, sauté green pepper in butter until tender.
3. Blend in flour, pimento, and mustard. Let simmer a few minutes.
4. Add cream, mayonnaise, and sherry to skillet. Gently fold in crabmeat.
5. Bake in a greased casserole for 20 minutes or in greased muffin tins or custard cups for 15 minutes.

# Sautéed Shrimp

| | |
|---|---|
| 1/2 | teaspoon minced garlic |
| 1 | tablespoon olive oil |
| 8 | ounces shrimp, peeled and deveined |
| 1 | tablespoon chopped fresh basil or 1 teaspoon dried basil |
| | salt to taste |
| 1/8 | teaspoon ground pepper |

1. In a frying pan over low heat, sauté garlic in oil until garlic is golden.
2. Add shrimp and turn up heat slightly.
3. Cook, stirring, about 3 to 5 minutes, until shrimp are opaque and pink.
4. Stir in basil and remove from heat.
5. Season with salt and pepper and serve over rice or noodles.

**Variations**
Possible substitutions include butter instead of olive oil and parsley or marjoram instead of basil. Onion and/or dry white wine might be added.

# Shrimp Creole

1/2    **cup chopped onion**

3/4    **cup sliced celery**

1    **tablespoon butter**

1/4    **cup chopped bell pepper**

16    **ounces canned diced tomatoes**

5    **ounces Rotel tomatoes and green chilies**

1    **tablespoon sugar**

1/2    **teaspoon ground black pepper**

1    **tablespoon cornstarch**

2    **tablespoons cold water**

1    **pound shrimp, peeled and deveined**

2    **tablespoons chopped parsley**

1    **cup cooked rice**

1. In a large skillet with a lid, over medium heat, cook onion and celery in butter for a few minutes.
2. Add bell pepper, tomatoes, Rotel, sugar, and pepper. Cover and let simmer for about 15 minutes.
3. Dissolve cornstarch in cold water and stir into mixture. Add shrimp and parsley and let simmer, uncovered, another 10 minutes. Stir several times.
4. Serve over rice.

**Variation**

If hotter, spicier food is desired, add an entire 10-ounce can of Rotel.

# Shrimp or Lobster Newburg

| | |
|---|---|
| 1¹⁄₂ | tablespoons butter |
| ¹⁄₂ | teaspoon paprika |
| ¹⁄₈ | teaspoon ground black pepper |
| 2 | teaspoons chopped shallots or 1 teaspoon chopped onion |
| | dash cayenne |
| ¹⁄₂ | pound shrimp, peeled and deveined, or ¹⁄₂ pound lobster chunks |
| ¹⁄₂ | cup heavy cream |
| 1 | egg yolk |
| 2 | tablespoons dry sherry |
| | toast or patty shells |

1. Melt butter in a saucepan and add paprika, ground pepper, shallots, and cayenne. Cook, stirring, for about 2 minutes, until shallots are transparent.
2. Add shrimp or lobster and cook and stir for 2 minutes. Remove seafood with a slotted spoon and set aside.
3. Add cream to pan and let simmer for 2 minutes.
4. In a bowl, combine egg yolk with 1 tablespoon of the cream mixture and whisk. Add to pan and stir well.
5. Let simmer for 1 minute. Do not boil. Add wine and seafood. Heat but do not boil.
6. Serve over toast or patty shells.

# Grilled Swordfish with Sherry Sauce

1½–2  pounds swordfish, 1 inch thick

3  tablespoons butter

¼  cup sliced green onion

½  teaspoon crushed garlic

4  teaspoons flour

⅓  cup sour cream

½  cup chicken broth

2  tablespoons dry sherry

1. Place swordfish on a greased grill over medium-hot coals and let cook 5 minutes. Spread 1 tablespoon of the butter on fish. Turn over and butter with an additional 1 tablespoon. Broil another 3 to 7 minutes, until meat flakes easily.
2. In a skillet, sauté onion and garlic in remaining butter over medium heat until tender. Stir in flour and let simmer until thick. Stir in sour cream and broth. Bring just to a boil. Stir in sherry and simmer another 1 to 2 minutes. Serve over fish.

# Marinated Salmon                                         marinate 2 to 4 hours

½  cup rye whiskey

½  cup soy sauce

⅓  cup vegetable oil

1  tablespoon ground pepper

1  tablespoon garlic powder

½  cup brown sugar

2  pounds salmon fillet

1. Combine all ingredients except salmon in a flat plastic or glass container. Add salmon, cover, and marinate 2 to 4 hours.
2. Remove salmon from marinade, wrap in aluminum foil, and barbecue or bake (at 350 degrees for about 20 minutes per inch of thickness).

**Note**

The easiest way to marinate fish is to use a resealable plastic bag.

# Salmon Steak with Cream Sauce

| | |
|---|---|
| 1 | pound salmon steak |
| 2 | teaspoons butter |
| 2 | tablespoons chopped onion |
| 1 | teaspoon crushed garlic |
| 1/4 | cup chopped fresh basil |
| 2 | tablespoons chopped fresh parsley |
| 1/4 | cup dry white wine |
| 1 | teaspoon lime juice |
| 3 | tablespoons light cream |
| | dash of ground pepper |

1. Wash and dry salmon with paper towels.
2. In a medium-hot skillet, sauté salmon in butter until it flakes. Remove to a plate and keep warm.
3. Add onion and garlic to pan and reduce heat. Sauté until clear. Add remaining ingredients and simmer until mixture is slightly thickened. Pour over salmon and enjoy.

# Skillet Salmon with Curry

This is a gourmet dish that takes only a few minutes to prepare.

| | |
|---|---|
| 1 1/2 | pounds salmon fillet, 1/2-inch thick |
| 2 | tablespoons butter |
| 8 | ounces canned crushed pineapple, unsweetened |
| 1/2 | teaspoon curry powder |
| 1/4 | cup coarsely chopped roasted bell pepper |
| 1/2 | cup cream |
| 1 | tablespoon rum |

1. In a skillet, sauté salmon in butter over medium heat for 3 to 5 minutes, turning once. Transfer salmon to a serving plate immediately and keep warm.
2. Add pineapple, curry, and roasted pepper to the skillet and cook for just a minute. Add cream and let simmer for 2 to 3 minutes. Add rum. Stir well and pour over salmon.

# Baked Salmon with Almonds

1/4    cup butter, melted

1      cup bread crumbs

1/2    cup almonds, finely chopped

1      teaspoon grated lemon peel

2      tablespoons lemon juice

1/4    teaspoon salt

1/4    teaspoon pepper

1/4    cup chicken broth

2      pounds salmon fillets

1/4    cup sliced almonds

1. Preheat oven to 375 degrees.
2. In a bowl, combine 2 tablespoons of the butter with crumbs, chopped almonds, lemon peel, lemon juice, salt, and pepper. Mix well.
3. Pour broth into an 8 x 11-inch baking pan. Arrange salmon fillets in a single layer, skin-side down.
4. Pat bread crumb mixture over fillets, covering them as completely as possible. Drizzle remaining butter over all and sprinkle with sliced almonds.
5. Bake, uncovered, for 20 to 30 minutes. Test for flakiness. Topping should be golden.

# Shrimp Tacos

| | |
|---|---|
| 4 | 8-inch flour tortillas |
| 3/4 | pound medium-size shrimp, peeled and deveined |
| 1 | tablespoon olive oil |
| 1/2 | teaspoon minced garlic |
| 1/2 | teaspoon ground cumin |
| 1/2 | cup chopped onion |
| 1 | cup chopped tomatoes |
| 1/4 | cup fresh cilantro or celery leaves |
| 1/4 | teaspoon salt |
| 1 | jalapeño, seeded and finely chopped |
| | lime wedges |
| 1 | cup shredded Monterey Jack |
| 1/2 | cup sour cream |

1. Wrap tortillas in aluminum foil and warm in the oven for 10 minutes at 350 degrees.
2. In a skillet over medium heat, sauté shrimp in oil and garlic for 2 minutes. Add cumin and stir. Remove shrimp and set aside.
3. Add onion to skillet and cook until tender. Add tomatoes, cilantro, salt, and jalapeño. Cook for another 2 to 4 minutes. Add shrimp and heat through.
4. Spoon shrimp mixture into center of tortillas. Squeeze lime wedges over mixture and top with cheese and sour cream. Fold tortillas in half.

# Baked Clams

| | |
|---|---|
| 4 | dozen cherrystone clams |
| 1/4 | cup olive oil |
| 1/2 | teaspoon minced garlic |
| 1/4 | teaspoon ground pepper |
| 2 | tablespoons chopped fresh parsley |
| 1 | cup bread crumbs |
| 2 | tablespoons grated Parmesan |

1. Preheat oven to 375 degrees.
2. Shuck and clean clams. Finely chop, return to shells, and place in a shallow baking pan.
3. Combine remaining ingredients to make topping. Place about 1 tablespoon of topping on each clam.
4. Bake 12 to 15 minutes, until golden. Serve immediately.

## Note

These can be an appetizer as well as a main dish.

# VEGETABLES

# About Vegetables

Having covered many of the basic vegetable recipes in the first volume of *The Charlottesville Collection*, I have tried to find more original recipes for inclusion in this second volume. For example, you will find a number of sweet potato recipes here. I realized only recently how much more nutritious sweet potatoes are than white potatoes. (I prefer the light-colored sweet potatoes, when available; they are not as moist as yams.) You will also find several recipes for spinach, another particularly wholesome vegetable. My hope is that family cooks will be encouraged to incorporate more spinach and sweet potatoes into the family diet.

I often cook my vegetables in a steamer basket or microwave, which preserves the nutritious juices. If, however, you boil your vegetables, save the water for soup if you are going to make it within a day or two.

# Wild Mushroom Strudel

**Copper Mine Restaurant, Wintergreen Resort**
*Michael Miles, Chef*

| | |
|---|---|
| 1 | pound oyster mushrooms, sliced |
| 1 | pound shiitake, sliced |
| 1 | pound  domestic mushrooms, sliced |
| 1 | teaspoon (1 ounce) chopped shallots |
| 1 | teaspoon chopped garlic |
| 1/2 | cup (4 ounces) white wine |
| | salt and pepper to taste |
| 1/2 | teaspoon (.25 ounces) dried tarragon leaves |
| 1/2 | cup (6 ounces) heavy cream |
| 2 | sheets phyllo dough |

1. Preheat oven to 400 degrees.
2. Combine all ingredients except heavy cream and phyllo in a saucepan and sauté until shallots are translucent.
3. Add heavy cream and boil, stirring, until reduced by three quarters. Remove from heat and let cool.
4. Spoon 3 ounces of cooked mushroom mixture onto each phyllo sheet and roll up. Cook for 7 minutes, until golden brown.

# Sugar Snap Peas with Mint

$^1/_2$   cup water

$1^1/_2$   cups sugar snap peas, stem ends removed

1   tablespoon butter

2   tablespoons finely chopped fresh mint leaves

salt and pepper to taste

1. Put water in a small saucepan and cook peas, covered, over medium heat about 5 minutes, until crisp-tender. Drain immediately.
2. Add butter, mint, salt, and pepper and continue to cook, uncovered, for 1 or 2 minutes. Mix until peas are well coated.

**Yield: 3 servings**

# Citrus Beets                                    marinate 2 to 3 hours

$^1/_4$   cup orange juice

1   tablespoon cornstarch

$^1/_4$   cup lime juice

$^1/_4$   cup sugar

2   cups $^1/_2$-inch cubes cooked beets

$^1/_8$   teaspoon grated nutmeg

$^1/_2$   teaspoon salt

1   cup orange sections

1. In a saucepan, blend orange juice and cornstarch.
2. Add lime juice and sugar and cook over low heat until thickened. Add beets, nutmeg, salt, and orange sections. Let simmer for 5 minutes, stirring well.
3. Marinate for several hours before serving hot.

**Variation**

Substitute lemon juice for lime juice.

# Spicy Green Beans

- ¹/₂    **cup chopped onion**
- 1    **tablespoon minced green chilies**
- 1    **teaspoon minced garlic**
- 2    **tablespoons olive oil**
- ¹/₂    **pound green beans, stemmed and frenched (sliced lengthwise; see note)**
- ¹/₄    **cup diced fresh tomato**
- ¹/₂    **cup water**
-    **salt to taste**

1. In a skillet over medium heat, sauté onion, chilies, and garlic in oil until onion is translucent.
2. Add beans, tomato, and water. Cover and simmer for about 15 minutes, stirring occasionally, until beans are tender. Add salt to taste.

**Note**

Frenched beans cook more quickly and absorb flavors more efficiently.

# Stewed Tomatoes

- 16    **ounces canned whole tomatoes, undrained**
- 1    **tablespoon cornstarch**
- 1    **cup thinly sliced onion**
- 2    **tablespoons butter**
- 2    **teaspoons sugar**
-    **salt and pepper to taste**

1. Drain juice from tomatoes and mix juice with cornstarch.
2. In a saucepan, sauté onion in butter until translucent and tender.
3. Add tomatoes to saucepan. Add cornstarch mixture and sugar. Stirring continuously, bring to a gentle boil. When slightly thickened, remove from heat.
4. Season with salt and pepper and serve.

**Yield: 3 to 4 servings**

# Crunchy Cheese-Topped Tomatoes

| | |
|---|---|
| 1 | cup seasoned stuffing |
| 1 | tablespoon dried chives |
| 1/2 | cup shredded Cheddar |
| 1/8 | teaspoon ground pepper |
| 1/4 | cup melted butter |
| 4 | underripe tomatoes, halved |

1. Preheat oven to 350 degrees.
2. Combine stuffing, chives, cheese, and pepper. Stir in butter and mix well.
3. Line a baking pan with foil and place tomato halves in it. Spoon about 2 tablespoons of the crumb mixture onto each half.
4. Bake for about 15 minutes, until tomatoes are tender and topping is golden.

# Fried Green Tomatoes

This is an old-time Southern favorite.

| | |
|---|---|
| 4 | medium green tomatoes (see note) |
| | salt and pepper to taste |
| | cayenne to taste (optional) |
| 1/3 | cup flour |
| 2 | tablespoons cornmeal |
| 1/4 | cup vegetable oil |

1. Slice tomatoes into 1/4-inch slices. Sprinkle both sides of each with salt, pepper, and cayenne.
2. In a shallow bowl, combine flour and cornmeal.
3. Heat oil in a skillet until hot but not smoking. Dip tomato slices in cornmeal mixture, making sure to coat each side.
4. Fry a few at a time in the hot fat, about 3 minutes for each side, until golden. Drain on paper towels. Serve immediately.

**Note**
Make sure the tomatoes are firm and green all over.

# Red Cabbage Caraway

| | |
|---|---|
| 2 | pounds red cabbage, cut into 2-inch wedges |
| 2 | Granny Smith apples, peeled and diced |
| 1/4 | cup apple cider |
| 2 | tablespoons butter |
| 1/2 | teaspoon caraway seeds |
| 1/4 | teaspoon nutmeg |
| 2 | teaspoons sugar |
| 1/4 | teaspoon salt |
| 1/4 | cup red wine |

1. In a steamer pot, cook cabbage until crisp-tender.
2. Combine remaining ingredients except wine in a skillet and cook over medium heat for 15 to 20 minutes, until apples are mushy and mixture is thickened as a sauce. Add red wine. Let simmer a few minutes more.
3. Place cabbage in a casserole dish and pour sauce over, coating as completely as possible. Let sit in a warm (250-degree) oven for a few minutes, until flavors are absorbed, and serve.

# Creamed Brussels Sprouts

| | |
|---|---|
| 2 | cups brussels sprouts, fresh or frozen |
| 2 | tablespoons butter |
| 1 | tablespoon flour |
| 1 | cup milk (2% or richer) |
| 1/2 | teaspoon salt |
| 1/2 | teaspoon pepper |

1. Boil or steam fresh brussels sprouts until just tender, 10 to 12 minutes. Follow package directions to cook frozen sprouts. Drain well.
2. In a saucepan, melt butter and add flour. Cook for 2 to 3 minutes over medium-high heat. Add milk slowly, stirring briskly, until thickened.
3. Add brussels sprouts and simmer for 5 to 10 minutes, stirring occasionally. Season with salt and pepper and serve.

# Baked Cheese Cabbage

This dish is different—and really good.

|     |                         |
|-----|-------------------------|
| 4   | cups shredded cabbage   |
| 4   | tablespoons butter      |
| 1½  | tablespoons flour       |
| 1   | cup milk                |
| ¼   | teaspoon salt           |
| ¼   | teaspoon pepper         |
| 1¼  | cups shredded Cheddar   |
| 1½  | cups bread crumbs       |

1. Preheat oven to 350 degrees.
2. Steam cabbage for 3 to 4 minutes, until crisp-tender.
3. In a saucepan, melt 2 tablespoons of the butter, stir in flour, and gradually add milk. Stir well. Season with salt and pepper to taste.
4. Layer cabbage in a casserole. Top with a layer of cheese and then a layer of sauce.
5. Combine crumbs and remaining butter and sprinkle on top. Bake for 25 to 30 minutes.

# Carrots with Parsley

|   |                                      |
|---|--------------------------------------|
| 3 | cups baby carrots, halved lengthwise |
| 1 | cup water (approximate)              |
| 1 | tablespoon butter                    |
| 2 | teaspoons lemon juice                |
| 3 | tablespoons finely chopped fresh parsley |

1. In a small skillet, simmer carrots in the water and butter for about 15 minutes, until almost all water has evaporated and carrots are tender.
2. Add lemon juice and parsley. Toss and simmer 5 minutes more.

# Glazed Onions

| | |
|---|---|
| 1 | pound baby white onions |
| 4 | tablespoons butter |
| 1½ | tablespoons honey |
| | salt to taste |

1. Cook onions in a pot of water for 5 minutes over medium heat. Drain and peel.
2. In a skillet, melt butter and stir in honey. Add onions and cook over medium heat for 10 to 15 minutes, until onions are slightly browned. Add salt if desired.


# Cheese Cauliflower Casserole

| | |
|---|---|
| 1 | medium head cauliflower, broken into flowerets |
| 3 | tablespoons butter |
| 3 | tablespoons flour |
| 1¼ | cups milk |
| 1 | cup shredded sharp Cheddar |
| ½ | teaspoon salt |
| ¼ | teaspoon ground pepper |

1. Preheat oven to 350 degrees.
2. Steam cauliflower in a steamer basket until crisp-tender. Transfer to a casserole.
3. In a skillet, melt butter, stir in flour, and gradually add milk. When sauce has thickened, add cheese and stir until melted and well combined.
4. Top cauliflower with cheese sauce and bake for 20 to 30 minutes. Season with salt and pepper.

# Corn Fritters

1    egg
2    tablespoons milk
2    tablespoons flour
1½  cups corn kernels, fresh or frozen
1    tablespoon butter, melted
½   teaspoon salt
¼   teaspoon pepper

1. In a bowl, whisk egg until foamy. Whisk in remaining ingredients.
2. Drop by the tablespoonful onto a hot, greased griddle or into a heavy frying pan. Turn with a spatula as needed until cooked through. Serve with syrup and butter.

**Yield: 4 to 6 servings**

# Spinach-Stuffed Zucchini

1    large (about 1 pound) zucchini
1    package (10 ounces) frozen chopped spinach, cooked and well drained
2    tablespoons flour
½   cup milk
¼   teaspoon pepper
¼   teaspoon salt
½   cup shredded Cheddar
4    slices bacon, cooked and crumbled

1. Preheat oven to 350 degrees.
2. Trim the ends off the zucchini and boil whole for about 10 minutes. Drain.
3. Carefully, halve zucchini lengthwise. Scoop out the center, leaving a ½-inch shell all around, and reserve.
4. Place pulp, including seeds, in a saucepan and break into small pieces. Add spinach. Combine flour and milk and add to saucepan. Add pepper and salt and simmer until thickened, stirring often.
5. Place zucchini halves in a baking pan and fill them with spinach mixture. Sprinkle with cheese and bacon. Bake for 20 minutes.

# Mock Crab Cakes

I found this recipe down on the Chesapeake. Some locals claimed they couldn't tell whether the cakes contained crabmeat or not.

| | |
|---|---|
| 2 | cups coarsely grated zucchini (about 2 large zucchini) |
| 2 | eggs, lightly beaten |
| 1 | cup fine bread crumbs |
| 3 | green onions, chopped |
| 2½ | teaspoons Old Bay seasoning |
| 1 | teaspoon mayonnaise |
| ¼ | cup bread crumbs |
| | vegetable oil for frying |

1. Drain zucchini between paper towels until quite dry. This is very important.
2. Combine all ingredients except ¼ cup bread crumbs and vegetable oil in a large bowl. Mix well.
3. Pat into eight rounds and dust with bread crumbs.
4. Add oil to a heavy skillet until it is about ½ inch deep. Fry patties over medium-high heat for 2 minutes on each side. Drain on paper towels and serve.

# Zucchini Combo

| | |
|---|---|
| 4 | cups sliced zucchini |
| 2 | cups chicken broth |
| 1 | can (14$^1$/$_2$ ounces) diced tomatoes |
| 2 | tablespoons tomato paste |
| 1 | teaspoon minced garlic |
| 1 | cup diced onions |
| $^1$/$_2$ | cup chopped fresh parsley |
| $^1$/$_2$ | teaspoon oregano |

1. In a large saucepan over medium heat, cook zucchini in broth until crisp-tender. Drain and reserve juices for soup or other use.
2. In a separate pan, cook the remaining ingredients over medium heat for 20 to 30 minutes, until sauce thickens slightly.
3. Combine zucchini and tomato sauce and serve.

**Yield: 4 to 8 servings**

# Swiss Cheese and Vegetable Casserole

| | |
|---|---|
| 1 | bag (16 ounces) frozen broccoli, carrots, and cauliflower, thawed and drained |
| 1 | can (10$^3$/$_4$ ounces) cream of mushroom or chicken soup |
| $^1$/$_3$ | cup sour cream |
| $^1$/$_4$ | teaspoon pepper |
| 1 | jar (4 ounces) chopped pimento, drained |
| 1 | cup shredded Swiss cheese |
| 1 | can fried onions |

1. Preheat oven to 350 degrees.
2. Combine vegetables with soup, sour cream, pepper, pimento, $^1$/$_2$ cup of the cheese, and half the onions.
3. Pour into a casserole and bake, covered, for 35 minutes.
4. Top with remaining cheese and onions. Bake, uncovered, for another 5 minutes.

# Mashed Potato Casserole

marinate 24 hours

2¹/₂   **pounds potatoes, peeled**

1   **cup reduced-fat sour cream**

8   **ounces Neufchâtel or cream cheese, softened**

1   **teaspoon onion salt**

1   **teaspoon garlic salt**

2   **teaspoons butter**

¹/₂   **teaspoon paprika**

1. Boil potatoes until soft.
2. In a large mixing bowl, cream sour cream and cream cheese. Add potatoes and beat until light and fluffy. Add onion salt and garlic salt toward the end of the process.
3. Turn into a 2-quart casserole, dot with butter, and sprinkle with paprika.
4. Refrigerate for 24 hours.
5. Bake at 350 degrees for 45 minutes.

**Yield: 8 to 10 servings**

**Note**

This casserole freezes well. If frozen, bake at 350 degrees for 1³/₄ hours.

# Scalloped Potatoes with Cheese

| | |
|---|---|
| $1/2$ | cup chopped onion |
| 2 | tablespoons butter |
| 3 | tablespoons flour |
| $1^{1}/_2$–2 | cups milk |
| $1/2$ | cup shredded Cheddar plus extra for topping |
| $1/2$ | teaspoon salt |
| $1/2$ | teaspoon pepper |
| 3–4 | cups thinly sliced, peeled potatoes |

1. Preheat oven to 350 degrees.
2. In a saucepan over medium heat, sauté onion in butter until translucent. Add flour and stir well. Slowly add milk and stir until thickened. Add cheese, salt, and pepper.
3. Layer potatoes in a greased casserole. Top with sauce and a sprinkle of cheese if desired.
4. Cover and bake for 45 minutes. Uncover and bake for another 30 minutes, until potatoes are tender when tested with a fork.

## Note

The sauce also can be prepared in the microwave. Combine onion and butter in a 1-quart Pyrex measuring cup and microwave at high for 1 minute. Stir in flour and milk and microwave at high for 1 minute. Stir, add cheese, and microwave 1 to 2 minutes, until sauce is thickened and cheese melted.

## Variations

Add cubed ham or sliced hot dogs.

If you omit the cheese and don't add meat, add another $1/4$ teaspoon of salt.

# Potatoes Anna

¼ cup butter, melted
½ cup finely chopped onion
½ cup grated Parmesan
2 cups ⅛-inch, peeled potato slices
2 tablespoons chopped parsley

1. Preheat oven to 350 degrees.
2. Combine butter, onion, and cheese in a small bowl.
3. Place one layer of potatoes in a greased pie plate. Top evenly with one quarter of the cheese mixture. Add another layer of potatoes and top with another quarter of the cheese mixture. Repeat process until potatoes are used up, ending with cheese mixture.
4. Cover with aluminum foil and bake for 30 minutes.
5. Remove foil and bake another 30 minutes. Pour off excess butter or blot with paper towels. Garnish with parsley and serve.

# Stuffed Sweet Potatoes

3 medium sweet potatoes
½ cup drained crushed pineapple
2 tablespoons brown sugar
¼ cup butter
  pinch grated nutmeg

1. Bake potatoes at 350 degrees for about 40 minutes, until tender. Halve lengthwise and scoop out most of the pulp.
2. Mix pulp with pineapple, brown sugar, and butter. Refill the skins and sprinkle with nutmeg.
3. Bake for 15 to 20 minutes, until heated through.

# Dixieland Sweet Potato Casserole

|       |                                              |
|-------|----------------------------------------------|
| 2     | eggs                                         |
| 3     | cups cooked, mashed sweet potatoes           |
| 1/2   | cup sugar                                    |
| 2–3   | tablespoons sherry                           |
| 2     | tablespoons butter, melted                   |
| 1/4–1/2 | cup milk (use larger amount for dry potatoes) |
| 1/2   | teaspoon salt                                |

Topping:

|     |                            |
|-----|----------------------------|
| 1   | cup brown sugar            |
| 1/3 | cup flour                  |
| 3   | tablespoons butter, melted |
| 1/2 | cup pecans, chopped        |

1. Preheat oven to 350 degrees.
2. Beat eggs in a large bowl with an electric mixer. Beat in remaining casserole ingredients and continue beating until creamy. Pour into a greased casserole dish.
3. Combine topping ingredients in a bowl. Spread on top of the casserole.
4. Bake for 45 minutes.

**Note**

This casserole is good without the topping, too.

# Pineapple Sweets

This is a real winner—very easy and without all the calories of most sweet potato casseroles. It's plenty sweet!

>   3   sweet potatoes, cooked and skinned
>   1   can (8 ounces) crushed pineapple
>   1/4   cup orange juice

1. Preheat oven to 350 degrees.
2. Slice sweet potatoes into a small casserole or shallow dish.
3. Pour crushed pineapple and orange juice over potato slices.
4. Bake for 20 to 30 minutes.

# Whipped Sweet Potatoes

>   3   large sweet potatoes
>   1/4   cup butter
>   1/2   teaspoon cinnamon or nutmeg
>   1/4–1/2   cup milk (see note)

1. Boil sweet potatoes with skin on over medium heat for 20 to 30 minutes, until cooked through. Scoop pulp from skins and place in a bowl.
2. Add butter, cinnamon or nutmeg, and about half the milk to the bowl. Beat with an electric beater. Add milk gradually, until potatoes are light but not soggy. Serve immediately.

**Note**
The texture of sweet potatoes varies greatly. Add more milk for drier potatoes.

# Fried Sweet Potatoes

2–3   cooked sweet potatoes

1   tablespoon butter or olive oil

1/4   teaspoon cinnamon

    salt and pepper to taste

1. Peel potatoes and cut, either lengthwise or across, into ½-inch slices.
2. Sauté in butter or oil over medium-high heat until both sides are lightly browned. Sprinkle with seasonings and serve immediately.

## Note

A quick and easy way to serve leftover baked or boiled sweet potatoes.


# Yellow Squash

This is a great and easy way to prepare squash that's just a bit different.

1   pound yellow squash, sliced into ½-inch rounds

2   tablespoons olive oil

2   tablespoons chopped fresh basil leaves

1/2   teaspoon salt

1/4   teaspoon pepper

2   tablespoons grated Parmesan

1. Steam squash in a steamer basket for 2 to 3 minutes, until just tender.
2. In a saucepan over medium-high heat, heat olive oil and basil for 1 minute. Add salt and pepper. Add squash and mix gently.
3. Place in a serving dish and sprinkle with Parmesan.

## Notes

I once used dried basil; we had had a frost, and fresh basil wasn't available. It worked very well. Just use one third as much dried basil as fresh.

# California Squash Casserole

| | |
|---|---|
| 2 | pounds yellow squash, thinly sliced |
| 1 | large onion, thinly sliced |
| 1/4 | cup butter |
| 2 | tablespoons flour |
| 1 | teaspoon dill weed |
| 1 | teaspoon salt |
| 1/4 | teaspoon ground pepper |
| 3 | eggs |
| 1 1/2 | cups milk |
| 1 | cup shredded Monterey Jack |
| 1 | cup crushed cracker crumbs |
| 2 | tablespoons butter, melted |

1. Preheat oven to 325 degrees.
2. In a saucepan over medium heat, sauté squash and onion in butter until soft.
3. Stir in flour, dill, salt, and pepper until well blended. Spoon into 8-cup casserole.
4. Beat eggs and combine with milk. Pour over squash mixture and sprinkle with cheese.
5. Bake for 40 minutes. Toss cracker crumbs with butter and sprinkle over casserole. Bake another 10 minutes.

# Grecian Eggplant

| | |
|---|---|
| 1 | pound eggplant |
| 1/2 | cup sliced onion |
| 2 | tablespoons olive oil |
| 3/4 | cup chopped, roasted red pepper |
| 1 | tablespoon brown sugar |
| 3 | tablespoons wine vinegar |
| 1/2 | teaspoon dried oregano |
| | salt and pepper to taste |
| 1/4 | cup chopped black olives |
| 1/3 | cup crumbled feta |

1. Bake eggplant at 425 degrees for 30 minutes. Peel and cube.
2. In a large saucepan, sauté onion in olive oil for just a minute, until translucent. Add pepper, brown sugar, vinegar, and oregano. Cook slowly over low heat for 5 minutes to mingle flavors.
3. Add cubed eggplant and salt and pepper to taste. Heat thoroughly.
4. Toss with olives and feta.

**Yield: 4 servings**

Some say that Vinegar Hill, on the northwest corner of Charlottesville's downtown mall, was named after Vinegar Hill in Enniscorthy, Ireland, site of a 1798 Catholic uprising. In spite of evidence that the name was in use during the nineteenth century, others say it came from the thriving bootleg whiskey business carried on there in the early 1900s, when bootleggers put vinegar labels on the whiskey jars.

# Vegetable Pie

Crust:

| | |
|---|---|
| 2 | cups wheat germ |
| $1/4$ | cup grated Parmesan |
| 4 | tablespoons melted butter |

Filling:

| | |
|---|---|
| $1/2$ | teaspoon minced garlic |
| 2 | tablespoons butter |
| $1^1/_2$ | cups thinly sliced zucchini |
| $1/2$ | teaspoon dried marjoram |
| $2/3$ | cup chopped bell pepper |
| 2 | cups chopped fresh tomato |

Topping:

| | |
|---|---|
| 2 | cups shredded Monterey Jack |

1. Preheat oven to 350 degrees.
2. Mix crust ingredients well and pat into a 9-inch pie pan. Set aside.
3. In a saucepan over medium heat, sauté garlic in butter for about 1 minute. Add zucchini, marjoram, and pepper and sauté for about 5 minutes, until pepper is crisp-tender.
4. Add tomato. Cover pan and cook another 5 minutes.
5. Spoon filling, liquid and all, into crust. Sprinkle with cheese and bake for 25 minutes.
6. Cut into pie-shaped wedges.

**Yield: 8 servings**

# BREADS

# About Breads

The more I bake, the more I realize how important the type of flour is to breads. Different kinds of flour have different gluten contents and affect the outcome of baking. The best yeast breads are made from bread flour, which is high in gluten and makes a good dough for rising. Biscuits do better with Southern biscuit flour, which is now available at many grocery stores. As for all-purpose flour, I prefer unbleached.

The whole grain flours are very nutritious and can substitute, at least in part, for other flours in most recipes. However, the substitution of whole grain flour can make breads more coarse. Up to half the white flour can be replaced by whole wheat flour without substantially changing the texture of breads and pastries. Just increase the liquid slightly and let the dough rest for 5 minutes before kneading. Nutritional value is increased and flavor enhanced.

Several types of yeast are available. I find that instant or Rapid Rise yeast speeds rising and mixing. It can be mixed with the flour and doesn't have to be dissolved first in warm water, though warm liquid does have to be added during mixing.

Finding a warm place to let the bread rise, which takes anywhere from 1 to 2 hours, was a challenge. I have found that a pan of hot water in the bottom of an unheated oven works best. It provides moisture and gentle warmth (about 80 degrees).

In quick breads, the substitution of unseasoned applesauce or mashed banana for some of the oil is generally satisfactory. I substitute for up to half the oil if I want to reduce calories.

Wrap your breads in a kitchen towel before heating or thawing them in the microwave. Doing so keeps the moisture evenly distributed. Fifty percent power is safest.

# Tavern Biscuits

## From the Ordinary at Michie Tavern, Circa 1784

| | |
|---|---|
| 2 | cups all-purpose flour |
| 2 | teaspoons baking powder |
| 1/4 | teaspoon salt |
| 3 | tablespoons shortening |
| 2/3 | cup whole milk |

1. Preheat oven to 450 degrees.
2. Sift together flour, baking powder, and salt. Cut in shortening with a pastry cutter. Stir in milk quickly with a fork to make dough light and fluffy but not sticky.
3. Knead until dough is smooth, about 20 times. Roll out on a lightly floured board and cut into biscuits 1/2-inch thick.
4. Bake on a greased cookie sheet for 12 to 16 minutes.

**Yield: 14 to 16 biscuits**

# Tavern Cornbread

**From the Ordinary at Michie Tavern, Circa 1784**

1 cup self-rising white cornmeal

1 cup sifted all-purpose flour

1/4 cup sugar

1 teaspoon salt

4 teaspoons baking powder

1 egg

1 cup milk

1/4 cup shortening, melted

2 tablespoons butter

1. Preheat oven to 425 degrees.
2. Sift cornmeal, flour, sugar, salt, and baking powder together in a large bowl. Add egg, milk, and shortening. Beat with an electric beater until smooth, about 1 minute.
3. Bake in a greased 8 x 8-inch pan for 20 to 25 minutes. Remove from oven and dot with butter while hot. Cut into squares and serve.

**Yield: 9 servings**

# Liscombe Lodge Brown Bread

I was served this loaf of bread on a fall visit to Liscombe, Nova Scotia. Chef Blaise MacInnis was kind enough to share his recipe with me. I hope you like it as much as I do. I did reduce the quantities so that it can be made easily in a regular mixing bowl. I usually double the recipe (and struggle with it a bit), then freeze the extra loaves.

| | |
|---|---|
| 3 | cups whole wheat flour |
| 2 | cups white bread flour |
| 1 | tablespoon Rapid Rise yeast |
| 1 | teaspoon salt |
| 3 | tablespoons canola oil |
| 1³/₄ | cups water |
| ¹/₂ | cup molasses |

1. Combine flours.
2. In a large mixing bowl, combine yeast, salt, and about half the flour mixture. Mix well.
3. In a 1-quart measuring cup, combine oil, water, and molasses. Heat in the microwave until warm but not hot, at medium for approximately 1 minute.
4. Pour molasses mixture slowly into flour and yeast mixture, stirring or beating it in. Slowly add as much of the flour blend from step 1 as seems workable for your mixer.
5. Remove to floured board and knead in remaining flour until dough is a fairly firm ball. Continue to knead for 6 to 8 minutes.
6. Place dough in a greased bowl and roll it around until lightly coated with grease. Cover with a warm, damp towel and place above a large pan of hot water in an unheated oven.
7. When dough has risen to twice its original size, remove it from the bowl. Punch down and knead just a couple of times. Divide in half and let rest for 10 minutes.
8. Form into 2 uniform loaves. Place in greased loaf pans, cover with a warm, damp towel, and let rise in a warm place for another 30 minutes.
9. Bake at 350 degrees for 35 to 40 minutes.

# Focaccia

Any combination of herbs and/or thinly sliced vegetables—crushed fresh rosemary, dried sage, dried tomato slices with oregano, fresh tomato slices with a bit of basil, black olive slices with small pieces of feta, or thin onion slices—or even cheeses can be added before this bread's second rising. My favorite is oregano and dried tomato slices.

| | |
|---|---|
| 1½ | cups whole wheat flour |
| 1–1½ | cups white bread flour |
| 1 | package Rapid Rise yeast |
| 1 | teaspoon sugar |
| 1 | teaspoon salt |
| 1 | cup hot water |
| 3 | tablespoons olive oil plus extra for oiling a baking sheet |
| 1 | teaspoon coarse salt |
| | herbs and/or vegetables |

1. In a large bowl, combine whole wheat flour, 1 cup of the white bread flour, yeast, sugar, and salt.
2. Combine water and 1 tablespoon of the olive oil and stir into flour mixture. Add more white bread flour if needed to make a soft ball of dough that pulls away from the bowl.
3. Knead the dough on a lightly floured board for 5 to 10 minutes.
4. Place in a greased bowl and grease the top. Cover with a warm, damp towel and let rise in a warm place for 1 to 1½ hours.
5. Punch down and knead for a few minutes. Stretch the dough into a 12 x 12-inch square or two 9-inch circles and place on a large baking sheet oiled with olive oil. Sprinkle course salt and herbs and/or vegetables on top.
6. Cover the sheet with a warm, damp cloth and let dough rise for another 45 minutes.
7. Make dents about every 2 inches with your fingertips. Drizzle remaining 2 tablespoons of olive oil over all.
8. Bake at 375 degrees for about 25 minutes, until golden.

# Italian Flatbread with Sage

| | |
|---|---|
| 1 | package Rapid Rise yeast |
| 1/2 | teaspoon salt |
| 1 1/2 | teaspoons dried sage |
| 2 1/4–2 1/2 | cups bread flour |
| 3/4 | cup hot water (about 125 degrees) |
| 3 | teaspoons olive oil |
| 1/4 | teaspoon kosher salt |

1. Preheat oven to 500 degrees.
2. In a food processor or mixer bowl, combine yeast, salt, 1 1/4 teaspoons of the sage, and 1 cup of the flour.
3. Turn on mixer or processor and slowly add water and 2 teaspoons of the olive oil.
4. Add another cup of flour and mix by hand or with a dough hook. Dough should form a soft ball. Turn it onto a floured board and knead in remaining flour until ball is no longer sticky.
5. On a greased baking sheet, pat dough into a round 1/2-inch thick. Prick it with a fork at 2-inch intervals. Brush with remaining oil and sprinkle with kosher salt and remaining 1/4 teaspoon of sage.
6. Bake dough for 13 to 15 minutes, until golden brown.

# Honey-Oatmeal Bread

| | |
|---|---|
| 2 | cups milk |
| 1/3 | cup honey |
| 1/4 | cup canola oil |
| 2 | teaspoons salt |
| 1 | tablespoon water |
| 2 1/2 | cups whole wheat flour |
| 3 | packages Rapid Rise yeast |
| 1/2 | cup quick-cooking oats plus additional for dredging |
| 2–3 | cups white bread flour |
| 1 | egg white, beaten |

1. In a saucepan over low heat, combine and warm milk, honey, oil, salt, and water.
2. In a large mixing bowl, combine 2 cups of the whole wheat flour with the yeast. Slowly add milk mixture.
3. Beat on low for 30 seconds. Beat on high for 3 minutes.
4. Stir in oats and add remaining whole wheat flour and sufficient white bread flour to make a pliable ball of dough. Turn out on a floured board and knead for 5 minutes.
5. Place in a greased bowl, grease the top, and cover with a warm, damp towel. Set in a warm place and let rise until it has doubled in bulk.
6. Return dough to the board and knead some more. Let rest for 10 minutes. Cut in half, place in greased loaf pans, and sprinkle with more oats. Let rise for another 1/2 hour.
7. Brush with egg white and bake at 375 degrees for 35 to 40 minutes.

# Almond Rolls

| | |
|---|---|
| 1 | package Rapid Rise yeast |
| 2 | cups all-purpose flour |
| 1/2 | teaspoon salt |
| 5 | tablespoons sugar |
| 3/4 | cup milk |
| 1/4 | cup butter |
| 3 | drops almond flavoring |
| 2 | eggs |
| 1 | cup almonds, blanched and chopped |

1. Combine yeast, flour, salt, and 1 tablespoon of the sugar in a large bowl.
2. In a saucepan over low heat, warm milk and add butter. Heat until quite warm but not hot (100–105 degrees).
3. Pour milk mixture into flour mixture. Add almond flavoring and stir well. Add eggs one at a time and beat well until smooth.
4. Cover dough with a warm, moist cloth and let rise in a warm place until it has doubled in bulk.
5. Punch down and add 1/2 cup of the almonds.
6. Half-fill greased muffin cups with the dough. Combine remaining 4 tablespoons of sugar and remaining 1/2 cup of almonds and sprinkle over the top of the rolls.
7. Put a warm, damp towel over all and let dough rise again until it has doubled in bulk.
8. Bake at 375 degrees for 15 to 20 minutes.

# Swedish Coffee Cake

| | |
|---|---|
| 3 | eggs, beaten |
| 2 | cups sugar |
| 1/2 | pound (2 sticks) butter |
| 3 | cups all-purpose flour |
| 1/4 | teaspoon salt |
| 3 | teaspoons baking powder |
| 12 | ounces evaporated milk |

Topping:

| | |
|---|---|
| 1/4 | cup brown sugar |
| 4 | tablespoons butter, melted |
| 4 | tablespoons all-purpose flour |
| 3/4 | cup shredded coconut or nuts (e.g., almonds) |

1. Preheat oven to 350 degrees.
2. In a large bowl, beat eggs, sugar, and butter together until well creamed.
3. Combine flour, salt, and baking powder in a bowl and add to the egg mixture alternately with evaporated milk. Mix well.
4. Pour into a greased 9 x 13-inch baking pan. Bake for 30 to 35 minutes.
5. Combine topping ingredients in a bowl.
6. When the cake has been baked and is still hot, spread with the topping. Broil for a few minutes, until topping is hot and bubbly.

**Yield: 10 to 12 servings**

# Raised Coffee Cake

| | |
|---|---|
| 1 | cup milk |
| 1/2 | cup plus 2 tablespoons butter |
| 1/2 | cup whole wheat flour |
| 3 | cups all-purpose flour |
| 1/3 | cup sugar |
| 1 | package Rapid Rise yeast |
| 1/2 | teaspoon salt |
| 1/4 | teaspoon almond flavoring |
| 1/4 | teaspoon ground cardamom |
| 1 | egg, beaten |
| 1 | cup cinnamon, raisins, brown sugar, and nuts of your choice (e.g., walnuts, hazelnuts, almonds) for filling (approximate) |

1. Scald milk and add 1/2 cup of butter to it. Let cool slightly.
2. Combine whole wheat flour, 2 1/2 cups of the all-purpose flour, sugar, yeast, salt, almond flavoring, and cardamom in a large bowl.
3. Pour warm milk mixture over dry ingredients. Mix well. Add and mix in egg.
4. Turn onto a floured board. Knead in enough of the remaining white flour to make a soft dough. Place in a greased bowl, cover with plastic, and let rise in a warm place until it doubles in bulk.
5. Return dough to floured board; punch down and knead again. Roll out to a 10 x 18-inch rectangle. Dot with 2 tablespoons butter. Fill with cinnamon, raisins, brown sugar, and nuts, roll up, and twist into a ring.
6. Put ring on a greased cookie sheet and let rise again for 1 hour. Bake at 350 degrees for 30 to 35 minutes.

## Note
If you use regular yeast, first dissolve it in 1/4 cup warm water and 1/2 teaspoon sugar. Reduce the milk to 3/4 cup.

## Variation
Fill with 1 jar of apricot preserves instead of brown sugar and nut mixture.

# Lemon Walnut Bread

| | |
|---|---|
| 3 | tablespoons butter |
| 1 | cup sugar |
| 2 | eggs |
| 1/2 | cup applesauce |
| 4 | teaspoons lemon juice |
| 1 | tablespoon grated lemon rind |
| 1 1/2 | cups all-purpose flour |
| 1 | teaspoon baking powder |
| 1/2 | cup milk |
| 3/4 | cup walnuts, chopped |
| 1/2 | cup confectioners' sugar |

1. Preheat oven to 350 degrees.
2. Cream butter and sugar. Beat in eggs one at a time.
3. Stir in applesauce, 1 teaspoon of the lemon juice, and rind.
4. Combine flour and baking powder.
5. Add flour mixture and milk alternately to the applesauce mixture. Stir in nuts.
6. Pour into a greased 5 x 9-inch loaf pan and bake for about 50 minutes.
7. Combine confectioners' sugar and remaining lemon juice and pour over the hot bread.

# Company Cornbread

| | |
|---|---|
| 1 | cup yellow cornmeal |
| 1 | cup all-purpose flour |
| 4 | tablespoons sugar |
| 2 | teaspoons cream of tartar |
| 1/4 | teaspoon salt |
| 1 | teaspoon baking soda |
| 1 | cup sour cream |
| 1/4 | cup milk |
| 2 | eggs, well beaten |
| 4 | tablespoons butter, melted |

1. Preheat oven to 425 degrees.
2. Combine cornmeal, flour, sugar, cream of tartar, salt, and baking soda in a large bowl.
3. Add sour cream, milk, eggs, and butter and stir until just moist. Do not overmix.
4. Spoon batter into a 9 x 9-inch greased baking pan. Bake for about 25 minutes.

**Note**

This recipe doubles very nicely, and the cornbread freezes well. It's a real winner!

# Buttermilk Biscuits

| | |
|---|---|
| 2 | teaspoons baking powder |
| 1 | teaspoon baking soda |
| 1 | teaspoon sugar |
| $1/2$ | teaspoon salt |
| $3^1/2$ | cups all-purpose flour |
| $1/4$ | pound butter |
| $1^1/2$ | cups buttermilk |

1. Preheat oven to 375 degrees.
2. Combine baking powder, baking soda, sugar, salt, and flour. Mix well.
3. Using a pastry cutter, cut in butter. Mixture should resemble coarse bread crumbs. Gently add buttermilk and mix.
4. On a lightly floured board, gently pat out dough. Cut with a cutter or glass into round biscuits.
5. Bake on an ungreased cookie sheet for about 10 minutes.

# Cranberry Muffins

| | |
|---|---|
| 1 | cup raw cranberries, chopped |
| $3/4$ | cup sugar |
| $3/4$ | cup buttermilk, slightly warm |
| 1 | egg, slightly beaten |
| $1/4$ | cup butter, melted |
| $2^1/4$ | cups all-purpose flour |
| $3/4$ | teaspoon baking soda |
| $1/4$ | teaspoon salt |

1. Preheat oven to 400 degrees.
2. Combine cranberries and $1/2$ cup of the sugar and set aside.
3. Mix buttermilk, egg, and butter together in a bowl.
4. Combine flour, baking soda, salt, and remaining sugar in a bowl. Add the buttermilk mixture, stirring gently until just moistened. Stir in the cranberries.
5. Spoon into greased muffin tins. Bake for about 20 minutes.

# Orange Bran Muffins

We were served these very special muffins on a recent trip to Australia. The chef, Laurent Pedamy, gave the recipe to me only when I said I was doing this cookbook. The Silky Oaks Lodge in the rain forest near Cairns is where you'll find him.

| | |
|---|---|
| 1/2 | cup golden raisins |
| 1/2 | cup coarsely chopped dried apple slices |
| 1/2 | cup fresh orange juice |
| 1 | cup unbleached all-purpose flour |
| 1 | teaspoon baking powder |
| 2 | teaspoons baking soda |
| 1/4 | teaspoon salt |
| 3/4 | cup sugar |
| 1/2 | teaspoon ground cinnamon |
| 2/3 | cup bran flake cereal |
| 1 | egg |
| 1/2 | cup milk |
| 1/3 | cup vegetable oil |

1. Combine raisins, dried apples, and orange juice. Set aside to soak for 30 minutes.
2. Preheat oven to 350 degrees. Line 16 cups in muffin tins with paper liners or butter them generously.
3. In a large bowl, sift together flour, baking powder, baking soda, salt, sugar, and cinnamon. Add bran cereal and mix well.
4. In another bowl, beat together egg, milk, and oil.
5. Make a well in the center of the dry ingredients and pour the egg mixture into it. Mix gently and add raisins, apples, and orange juice. Stir just until all ingredients are incorporated—do not overmix.
6. Fill each cup about three-quarters full with the batter and bake 18 to 20 minutes, until a toothpick comes out clean. Transfer muffins to a rack and let cool.

### Variation
Add 1/2 cup chopped dried apricots and/or 2 tablespoons finely chopped orange peel.

# Apple-Pecan Muffins

| | |
|---|---|
| 2 | cups peeled, cubed apples |
| 2 | large eggs |
| 3 | tablespoons applesauce |
| 3/4 | cup sugar |
| 1 1/2 | cups all-purpose flour |
| 2 | teaspoons baking powder |
| 1 1/2 | teaspoons ground cinnamon |
| 1 | teaspoon baking soda |
| 1/4 | teaspoon salt |
| 3 | tablespoons butter, melted |
| 1/2 | cup pecans, chopped |

1. Preheat oven to 400 degrees.
2. In a food processor, finely chop apples. Add eggs, applesauce, and sugar. Let stand for 10 minutes.
3. In a large bowl, whisk together flour, baking powder, cinnamon, baking soda, and salt.
4. Add the apple mixture to the flour mixture and stir gently. Add butter and pecans and stir until just moist. Do not overmix.
5. Pour batter into greased muffin pans and bake for about 15 minutes. Test with a toothpick for doneness.

## Note

I'm sure these muffins would be good even without the pecans.

# Banana Nut Muffins

| | |
|---|---|
| 1½ | cups white flour |
| ½ | cup whole wheat flour |
| 2 | teaspoons baking powder |
| ½ | teaspoon baking soda |
| 1 | teaspoon ground cinnamon |
| 1 | egg |
| 1¼ | cups mashed ripe banana |
| ¾ | cup dark brown sugar |
| 3 | tablespoons vegetable oil |
| 3 | tablespoons milk |
| 1 | teaspoon vanilla |
| 1 | cup chopped walnuts |

1. Preheat oven to 375 degrees.
2. Combine flours, baking powder, baking soda, and cinnamon in a bowl.
3. In another bowl, beat egg on slow speed. Add banana and brown sugar and mix well.
4. Add vegetable oil, milk, and vanilla to banana mixture. Slowly add flour blend and stir until just well mixed. Stir in walnuts.
5. Pour into greased muffin tins or 4-inch loaf pans and bake for 15 to 25 minutes, until a toothpick comes out clean.
6. Serve hot or cold.

**Note**

These muffins may be frozen.

# Quick Herb Bread

| | |
|---|---|
| 1 | loaf French bread or baguette |
| 1/2 | teaspoon paprika |
| 1/4 | teaspoon dried rosemary |
| 1/4 | teaspoon dried thyme |
| 1/4 | teaspoon dried marjoram |
| 1/4 | teaspoon salt |
| 1/2 | cup butter, softened |

1. Preheat oven to 400 degrees.
2. Slice bread diagonally at one-inch intervals, leaving the bottom intact.
3. In a bowl, combine seasonings and butter. Spread between the slices.
4. Wrap bread completely in foil. Bake 15 to 20 minutes, until hot all the way through. Fold back the foil and bake another 5 minutes to crisp the crust.

Edgar Allan Poe attended the University of Virginia's second session, in 1826. The poet and short-story writer is said to have had a penchant for long, solitary hikes out into the Albemarle County countryside. Poe's "A Tale of the Ragged Mountains," in which the protagonist embarks on a long ramble among the hills to the west and south of Charlottesville, is thought to reflect his life at the University.

# Apple Butter Bread

| | |
|---|---|
| 1 | cup butter, softened |
| 2 | cups brown sugar |
| 2 | eggs |
| 4 | cups all-purpose flour |
| 2 | teaspoons ground cinnamon |
| 2 | teaspoons ground nutmeg |
| 2 | teaspoons ground allspice |
| 1 | teaspoon ground cloves |
| 1/2 | teaspoon salt |
| 4 | teaspoons baking soda |
| 1 1/2 | cups buttermilk |
| 2 | cups apple butter |
| 1 | cup chopped pecans |

1. Preheat oven to 350 degrees.
2. In a large mixing bowl, cream butter and sugar. Add eggs and beat well.
3. Combine flour, spices, salt, and baking soda. Add to the sugar mixture alternately with the buttermilk. Mix well.
4. Stir in apple butter and nuts.
5. Spoon batter into two greased loaf pans. Bake for 1 hour.
6. Let cool on a rack for a few minutes before turning out. When completely cool, wrap in plastic and refrigerate or freeze.

# DESSERTS

# About Desserts

Included in this section are recipes for dessert sauces and frostings as well as recipes for the desserts themselves. You can mix and match according to taste.

Whipped cream freezes well. I freeze it in dollops on aluminum foil, then package it in resealable plastic bags for storage in the freezer. Whipped cream thaws in just a few minutes, and freezing it means you don't have to have fresh whipping cream always on hand.

Prepared, folded piecrusts are very hardy. They may be frozen and will thaw in only 20 minutes. Roll crusts with a rolling pin to make them thinner and flakier.

# Tarte au Noix

chill crust 2 hours

**Prospect Hill, The Virginia Plantation Inn**
*The Sheehan Family, Innkeepers*

Shortbread crust:

| | |
|---|---|
| 1/2 | cup unsalted butter |
| 1 | cup flour |
| 1/4 | teaspoon salt |

Filling:

| | |
|---|---|
| 3 | large eggs, beaten |
| 2 2/3 | cups dark brown sugar |
| 1/4 | cup unsalted butter, melted |
| 1 1/2 | teaspoons vanilla |
| 2 | cups walnut pieces |

1. Combine crust ingredients in a food processor and process until crumbly.
2. Add 2 tablespoons of water at a time (up to 6 tablespoons) and process until correct texture. Refrigerate until firm enough to line pan, about 2 hours.
3. Line an 11-inch tart pan with shortbread crust and partially bake at 400 degrees, about 15 minutes.
4. Preheat oven to 350 degrees.
5. In a medium bowl, combine eggs, sugar, butter, and vanilla. Pour into tart crust. Sprinkle evenly with walnuts.
6. Place tart in the middle of the oven with a rack above it. Bake for 45 minutes or until well done. After 20 minutes, you may need to cover the rack above the tart with aluminum foil to prevent the top from burning.

# Lemon-Raspberry Squares

**BRIX Marketplace**
*Karen Laetare, Chef/Owner*

Adapted from a recipe in *Picnics & Tailgates* (Williams-Sonoma Outdoors).

| | |
|---|---|
| 1³⁄₄ | cups plus ¹⁄₃ cup all-purpose flour |
| ¹⁄₂ | cup confectioners' sugar plus extra for dusting |
| ¹⁄₂ | teaspoon salt |
| 1 | cup chilled unsalted butter, cut into small pieces |
| 1 | teaspoon ice water |
| 1 | cup raspberry jam |
| 2 | cups granulated sugar |
| 2 | teaspoons lemon zest |
| 4 | eggs, well beaten |
| ³⁄₄ | cup lemon juice |

1.  Preheat oven to 350 degrees.
2.  Line a 9 x 13-inch baking pan with foil. Put 1³⁄₄ cups flour, ¹⁄₂ cup confectioners' sugar, and salt in a food processor and pulse until blended. Cut in chilled butter and process until dough begins to come together. Add ice water if dough is too dry.
3.  Press dough evenly over bottom of baking pan. Bake crust until lightly brown, about 20 minutes. Let cool for 30 minutes. Spread jam over, making sure it covers the crust completely, to the edge of the foil.
4.  In a medium-size bowl, whisk together granulated sugar, ¹⁄₃ cup flour, and lemon zest. Put eggs in a large bowl and slowly add flour mixture. Mix with an electric mixer until well blended. Add lemon juice and blend well.
5.  Beginning at the corners of the pan, pour the lemon mixture slowly and carefully over the jam. You do not want the layers to mix.
6.  Bake 25 to 30 minutes, until lemon topping is just set and center is still a little soft. Do not overbake. Let cool in the pan.
7.  Remove from pan and peel foil from baked crust. Cut into even squares or triangles and dust with confectioners' sugar.

**Yield: about 2 dozen squares**

# Susan's Pound Cake

This is the best pound cake I have ever eaten. Everyone in my family is of the same opinion.

1   cup butter, at room temperature
3   cups sugar
6   large eggs
1   teaspoon vanilla
1   teaspoon almond flavoring
3   cups unsifted flour plus extra for dusting
1   cup whipping cream, unwhipped and at room temperature
    Lemon Glaze (below)

1.  Grease large angel food cake or Bundt pan and line the bottom with a ring of waxed paper. Dust all with flour.
2.  In a large mixing bowl, cream butter and sugar and add eggs one at a time, beating well. Beat in vanilla and almond extract.
3.  Turn beater to low speed and mix in flour and whipping cream alternately.
4.  Pour batter into pan and place in a cold oven.
5.  Set oven for 375 degrees and bake 1½ hours.
6.  Let cool for 10 minutes and invert. Pour Lemon Glaze over cake and serve.

# Lemon Glaze

¼   cup lemon juice
1   teaspoon grated lemon peel
2   cups confectioners' sugar (approximate)

1.  In a pan over low heat, gently heat all ingredients until sugar dissolves, stirring all the while. If a thicker consistency is desired, add a bit more confectioners' sugar.
2.  Pour over cooled cake.

# Grandma's Chocolate Cake

| | |
|---|---|
| 3 | ounces unsweetened baking chocolate |
| 2 | cups milk |
| 4$\frac{1}{2}$ | tablespoons butter |
| 1$\frac{1}{2}$ | teaspoons vanilla |
| 1$\frac{1}{2}$ | teaspoons baking soda |
| 2$\frac{1}{2}$ | cups flour |
| 1$\frac{1}{2}$ | cups sugar |
| $\frac{1}{2}$ | teaspoon salt |
| | Chocolate Butter Cream Frosting (below) |

1. In a small saucepan over low heat, combine chocolate and 1 cup of the milk. Stir until smooth and slightly thickened. Add butter and stir until melted. Let cool. Stir in vanilla.
2. Preheat oven to 350 degrees. Grease and flour two round 9-inch cake pans.
3. Dissolve baking soda in remaining 1 cup of milk.
4. In a mixing bowl, combine flour, sugar, and salt. Add chocolate mixture and milk–baking soda mixture to the dry ingredients. Stir until batter is smooth.
5. Pour into cake pans and bake for 25 to 30 minutes. Let cool for 10 minutes. Remove from pans and continue to let cool on racks before frosting.
6. Frost with Chocolate Butter Cream Frosting.

# Chocolate Butter Cream Frosting

| | |
|---|---|
| 3 | ounces unsweetened chocolate |
| 6 | tablespoons butter, softened |
| 1 | teaspoon vanilla |
| 4 | cups confectioners' sugar |
| 4–6 | tablespoons milk |

1. Melt chocolate in a pan over heat or in the microwave. Scrape into a mixing bowl. Add butter and vanilla and mix with an electric beater.
2. Beat in sugar and milk alternately until frosting is of a consistency conducive to spreading.

**Yield: enough for the filling and frosting of a 9-inch, two-tier cake**

# Sunshine Cake

|   |   |
|---|---|
| 2 | eggs |
| 1 | teaspoon vanilla |
| 1 | cup granulated sugar |
| 1 | cup all-purpose flour |
| 1 | teaspoon baking powder |
| 1/2 | cup milk |
| 1 | tablespoon butter |
|   | Easy Nut Topping (below) |

1. Preheat oven to 350 degrees.
2. In a large bowl, beat eggs and vanilla until slightly thickened. Gradually add sugar and beat well.
3. Combine flour with baking powder and whisk into egg mixture to make smooth batter.
4. Combine milk and butter and heat in the microwave at medium for 1 minute. Stir into batter and mix well.
5. Pour batter into a greased 8 x 8-inch pan and bake for 25 minutes, until a toothpick comes out clean.
6. Ice with Easy Nut Topping or another favorite.

# Easy Nut Topping

|   |   |
|---|---|
| 3 | tablespoons butter |
| 3 | tablespoons dark brown sugar |
| 2 | tablespoons cream |
| 3/4 | cup chopped nuts (e.g., walnuts or hazelnuts) or shredded coconut |

1. Combine all ingredients in a 1-quart, microwavable bowl and microwave at high for 1 1/2 minutes, stirring once.
2. Spread over cake. Place under the broiler for 1 or 2 minutes, until slightly browned.

# About Angel Food Cake

Angel food cake is low in calories, easy to make (from a box), and easy to buy ready-made. It can be found in almost any grocery store. If you decide to make it from a box, try to find the kind with two packages—one for the egg whites and one for the flour. The cake will rise higher and taste better. When the ingredients are combined, the cake is one-step but inferior. Food Lion, for one, still carries the two-package kind.

All sorts of variations on the traditional angel food cake are delicious, unusual desserts that can be made in minutes. A few of the possibilities follow.

Serve it with sliced fruit in season or frozen fruit partially thawed. Raspberries are especially good, and angel food cake sprinkled with strawberries makes a good strawberry shortcake.

Serve it with ice cream and any fruit or sweet sauce, such as Apricot Sauce (page 262). Add whipped cream if you're not watching your weight. My favorite is vanilla ice cream and peaches or fudge sauce (variation, page 251).

Fill it with colored sherbets and ice it with whipped cream. The secret is to slice an inch off the top and then scoop out the cake in the middle to within three quarters of an inch of the sides. Scoop the sherbet into the void, replace the top slice, ice with the whipped cream, and freeze. Such a dessert will keep for many days in the freezer.

Serve it with chocolate or maple icing or with a drizzle of thin lemon icing.

## Heath Bar Angel Food Cake

refrigerate overnight and
chill additional 2 to 3 hours

1   pint whipping cream, unwhipped

4   tablespoons cocoa

1   cup confectioners' sugar

6   Heath bars

1   angel food cake

1.  Put cream in a bowl and mix in cocoa and confectioners' sugar. Let sit overnight in the refrigerator.
2.  Whip the cream. Place Heath bars between wax paper and crush with a rolling pin. Fold into the chocolate whipped cream.
3.  Using a bread knife, slice cake into 3 layers. Fill the layers and coat the outside with the chocolate cream. Chill in refrigerator for several hours.

# Fudge Frosting

| 2 | ounces unsweetened chocolate |
| $1\frac{1}{2}$ | cups sugar |
| $\frac{1}{2}$ | cup milk |
| 4 | tablespoons butter |
| 1 | tablespoon corn syrup |
| 1 | teaspoon vanilla |

1. In a heavy-bottomed pan, stir together all ingredients except vanilla.
2. Bring to a rolling boil, stirring continuously, and cook for 1 minute.
3. Let cool. Add vanilla and beat vigorously until frosting thickens.
4. Spread on a cooled cake immediately.

### Variation
If you add another $\frac{1}{4}$ cup milk, you'll have a great fudge sauce for ice cream.

# Butterscotch Sauce

| 1 | pound light brown sugar |
| $1\frac{2}{3}$ | cups light corn syrup |
| $\frac{3}{4}$ | cup butter |
| 13 | ounces evaporated milk |
| 1 | teaspoon vanilla |
| $\frac{1}{8}$ | teaspoon cream of tartar |

1. In a heavy saucepan, boil sugar, corn syrup, and butter over medium heat, stirring continuously, until it reaches the hard ball stage (250 to 266 degrees). .
2. Remove from heat and whisk in remaining ingredients. Beat well.
3. Serve on ice cream or unfrosted cakes. Keep covered in refrigerator for several months.

# Hershey's Kisses Cookies

chill 1 hour

|       |                             |
|-------|-----------------------------|
| 1     | cup butter, soft            |
| 2/3   | cup sugar                   |
| 1     | teaspoon vanilla            |
| 1²/3  | cups flour                  |
| 1/4   | cup cocoa                   |
| 1     | cup pecans, finely chopped  |
| 25    | Hershey's Kisses            |
| 1/2   | cup confectioners' sugar    |

1. Cream butter and sugar until light and fluffy. Stir in vanilla.
2. Combine flour and cocoa and blend into butter mixture. Stir in nuts.
3. Chill dough 1 hour. Preheat oven to 375 degrees.
4. Mold 1 tablespoon dough around each kiss, covering completely.
5. Place on ungreased cookie sheet and bake 10 to 12 minutes. When completely cooled, dust with confectioners' sugar.

# Chocolate Peanut Butter Bars

These delicious no-bake cookies are very easy to make and nutritious, too.

|       |                               |
|-------|-------------------------------|
| 1²/3  | cups graham cracker crumbs    |
| 2     | cups confectioners' sugar     |
| 1     | cup butter                    |
| 1     | cup crunchy peanut butter     |
| 6     | ounces semisweet chocolate chips |

1. Combine graham cracker crumbs and sugar in a bowl.
2. In a small glass bowl, microwave butter and peanut butter at medium until melted. Stir until smooth.
3. Stir the butter mixture into the crumb mixture and continue to stir until smooth. Pat into a 9 x 12-inch pan.
4. Melt chocolate chips in the microwave. Spread over peanut mixture and let cool.
5. Cut into 1-inch, bite-size bars.

# Easy Lemon Bars

| | |
|---|---|
| 1 | egg |
| 1/2 | cup plus 3 tablespoons butter, softened |
| 1/4 | cup sugar |
| 2 | tablespoons milk |
| 1 | teaspoon lemon zest |
| 1 1/4 | cups flour |
| 1/2 | teaspoon baking powder |
| 2 | teaspoons lemon juice |
| 3/4 | cup confectioners' sugar |

1. Beat egg, 1/2 cup butter, sugar, milk, and lemon zest together in a bowl.
2. Combine flour and baking powder in a 2-cup measuring cup. Stir into butter mixture. Stir in 1 teaspoon of the lemon juice.
3. Spread evenly in a greased 8 x 8 x 2-inch Pyrex baking dish.
4. Microwave at high 3 to 6 minutes, until firm. Let cool.
5. Beat 3 tablespoons butter, remaining 1 teaspoon of lemon juice, and confectioners' sugar until smooth.
6. Spread over cooled dough. Cut into bars.

# Lace Oatmeal Cookies

| | |
|---|---|
| 1/2 | cup butter |
| 1/2 | cup brown sugar |
| 1/2 | cup white sugar |
| 1 | large egg |
| 4 | teaspoons milk |
| 1 | teaspoon vanilla |
| 2/3 | cup flour |
| 1/2 | teaspoon cinnamon |
| 1/2 | teaspoon baking soda |
| 1/2 | teaspoon baking powder |
| 2/3 | cup shredded coconut |
| 1 1/2 | cups oatmeal |

1. Preheat oven to 350 degrees.
2. Combine butter and sugars in a bowl and beat until light.
3. Add egg, milk, and vanilla and beat well.
4. Combine flour, cinnamon, baking soda, and baking powder and add to sugar mixture. Mix well.
5. Fold in coconut and oatmeal.
6. Drop rounded teaspoonfuls on a greased cookie sheet. Bake for about 10 minutes.

**Yield: 2 to 3 dozen cookies**

# Peanut Butter Cookies

| | |
|---|---|
| 1/2 | cup butter |
| 1/3 | cup crunchy peanut butter |
| 1/2 | cup dark brown sugar |
| 1/4 | cup white sugar |
| 1 | egg, beaten |
| 1 1/4 | cups flour |
| 1/2 | teaspoon baking soda |
| 1/2 | teaspoon baking powder |
| 1/2 | teaspoon vanilla |

1. Preheat oven to 350 degrees.
2. Cream butter and peanut butter. As you beat, slowly add sugars and egg.
3. Combine flour, baking soda, and baking powder and add slowly to the butter mixture. Add vanilla.
4. Place teaspoonfuls of batter on an ungreased cookie sheet. Flatten with a fork or your fingers.
5. Bake for 10 to 12 minutes, until cookies are slightly brown on the underside. Let cool for a few minutes before removing from cookie sheet.

*Both the natural beauty of the surrounding countryside and the man-made beauty of Charlottesville combine to weave a tapestry of American history of which few other towns or cities can boast.*

**—John F. Kennedy**

# Apricot and Apple Oatmeal Munchies

Tasty low-fat cookies are hard to find. These are both low in fat and delicious.

| | |
|---|---|
| 1$^1$/$_2$ | cups rolled oats |
| $^3$/$_4$ | cup white flour |
| $^3$/$_4$ | cup whole wheat flour |
| $^1$/$_2$ | cup brown sugar |
| 1 | teaspoon baking powder |
| $^1$/$_4$ | teaspoon baking soda |
| $^1$/$_2$ | teaspoon salt |
| 3 | teaspoons cinnamon |
| $^1$/$_2$ | cup dried apricots, diced |
| 1 | cup peeled and diced Granny Smith apples |
| $^1$/$_2$ | cup golden raisins |
| 1 | egg, slightly beaten |
| $^1$/$_2$ | cup honey |
| $^1$/$_2$ | cup canola oil |
| $^1$/$_3$ | cup milk |

1. Preheat oven to 375 degrees.
2. In a large bowl, combine oats, flours, sugar, baking powder, baking soda, salt, and cinnamon. Fold in apricots, apples, and raisins.
3. In another bowl, combine egg, honey, oil, and milk. Stir into dry ingredients and mix well.
4. Drop rounded teaspoonfuls onto an ungreased baking sheet. Flatten dough until cookies are about 1 inch wide.
5. Bake for 10 to 12 minutes, until lightly golden. Let cool on a rack.

# Rhubarb-Pineapple Cobbler

let stand 1 hour

| | |
|---|---|
| 8 | ounces canned crushed pineapple |
| 6 | cups 1-inch slices fresh rhubarb |
| 1¼ | cups brown sugar |
| 2 | tablespoons cornstarch |
| 1 | tablespoon white sugar |
| 2 | teaspoons grated lemon peel |
| ⅔ | cup flour |
| ⅓ | cup butter (approximate) |

1. In a bowl, combine pineapple, rhubarb, and 1 cup of the brown sugar. Let stand 1 hour to extract juices.
2. Preheat oven to 350 degrees.
3. Drain juices into a measuring cup and add water or pineapple juice to make ⅔ cup. Pour into a saucepan and stir in cornstarch and white sugar. Cook, stirring, over medium-high heat until thickened.
4. Add juices to rhubarb-pineapple mixture and stir in lemon peel. Transfer all to a 2-quart baking pan.
5. In another bowl, combine flour and remaining ¼ cup brown sugar. Using a pastry blender or fork, cut in butter until mixture is crumbly.
6. Spread flour mixture over rhubarb and pineapple and bake for about 1 hour, until light brown and bubbly.

**Variation**

You may use frozen rhubarb. Thaw and drain it before combining with the pineapple.

# Broiled Pineapple

| | |
|---|---|
| 4 | ¹/₂-inch-thick slices fresh pineapple |
| 4 | heaping teaspoons brown sugar |
| 1¹/₂ | tablespoons butter, melted |
| 1¹/₂ | tablespoons shredded sweetened coconut |

1. Place pineapple slices in a greased 8 x 8-inch pan and sprinkle with brown sugar. Drizzle butter over each.
2. Broil pineapple about 4 inches from heat until topping is bubbling.
3. Sprinkle coconut over pineapple and return pan to broiler for about 30 seconds, until coconut is toasted.

# Bread Pudding with Lemon Sauce

| | |
|---|---|
| 3 | tablespoons butter, softened |
| 1 | loaf French bread, thinly sliced |
| ¹/₄ | cup raisins |
| 1 | teaspoon cinnamon |
| 2¹/₂ | cups milk |
| 3 | eggs, lightly beaten |
| ¹/₂–³/₄ | cup sugar |
| 1 | cup ricotta |
| 1 | teaspoon vanilla |
| | Lemon Sauce (page 259) |

1. Preheat oven to 350 degrees.
2. Butter bread slices on both sides and layer in a 2-quart casserole. The bread should half fill the casserole.
3. Sprinkle raisins and cinnamon over and around bread.
4. Combine remaining ingredients except Lemon Sauce. Mix well and pour over bread.
5. Let stand 5 minutes, enabling bread to soak up cheese mixture.
6. Place casserole in a pan of boiling water to a depth of about 1 inch. Place carefully in oven and bake for 55 to 60 minutes.
7. Serve with Lemon Sauce.

# Lemon Sauce

| | |
|---|---|
| 1 | cup sugar |
| 2 | tablespoons cornstarch |
| 2 | cups boiling water |
| 4 | tablespoons butter |
| 2–3 | tablespoons lemon juice |
| 1 | teaspoon grated lemon rind |

1. Combine sugar and cornstarch in a saucepan. Slowly add boiling water, stirring continuously.
2. Boil for 1 minute. Add butter and lemon juice and rind, stirring well.
3. Serve warm over bread pudding.

# Easy Chocolate Mousse          chill 2 hours

| | |
|---|---|
| 1 | envelope plain gelatin |
| 1/2 | cup hot, strong coffee |
| 1/4 | cup milk |
| 6 | ounces chocolate chips |
| 2 | egg yolks |
| 1 | tablespoon sugar |
| 1 | cup crushed ice |
| 1 | cup heavy cream |

1. Soak gelatin in coffee and milk for 5 minutes. Blend mixture in a blender for 20 seconds.
2. Put chocolate chips in a measuring cup and melt in the microwave at low for 1 minute. Add melted chips, egg yolks, and sugar to the blender and blend for 40 seconds.
3. Add crushed ice and heavy cream and blend for 20 seconds.
4. Pour into serving dishes and refrigerate for at least 2 hours before serving.

# June's Apricot Dessert

|  |  |
|---|---|
| 4 | ounces whipping cream |
| 1 | teaspoon vanilla |
| 2 | teaspoons sugar |
| 16 | ounces canned apricots, well drained |

1. Whip cream to stiff peaks, adding vanilla and sugar toward the end.
2. Fold apricots into whipped cream. Serve in glass dishes for an attractive presentation.

# Pistachio Ice Cream

|  |  |
|---|---|
| 2¼ | cups light cream |
| 1 | cup sugar |
| 6 | ounces pistachio nuts, shelled |
| 2 | cups boiling water |
| ½ | teaspoon rose water |
| 1 | teaspoon vanilla |
| ½ | teaspoon almond extract |
| 2 | cups whipping cream, unwhipped |

1. Place 1 cup of the light cream and ¾ cup of the sugar in a saucepan and heat slowly to dissolve sugar. Do not boil. Chill in refrigerator while preparing the rest of the recipe.
2. Place nuts in a bowl and blanch by adding boiling water. Let sit for 2 minutes. Discard water.
3. Remove outer covering from nuts. If you wish, toast nuts in the oven at 350 degrees for 10 minutes. Chop the kernels coarsely in a blender or food processor or crush in a mortar.
4. Place nuts in a bowl and add remaining 1¼ cups of the light cream, ¼ cup of the sugar, rose water, vanilla, and almond flavoring. Stir until sugar dissolves.
5. Mix in whipping cream and chilled mixture from step 1. Follow directions for your ice cream maker.

# Cranberry Mousse

  1    cup cranberry juice cocktail

  1    package (3 ounces) raspberry-flavored gelatin

16    ounces canned jellied cranberry sauce

  1    cup whipping cream, whipped

1. In a saucepan, bring cranberry juice to a boil. Add gelatin and stir over high heat until gelatin dissolves.
2. Remove pan from heat and stir in cranberry sauce. Let cool until thickened. Fold in whipped cream.
3. Spoon into serving dishes and chill until firm. Serve with additional whipped cream if desired.

**Yield: 6 to 8 servings**


# Cranberry Crumble

3    cups peeled and sliced Granny Smith apples

2    cups raw cranberries, sorted

1    cup sugar

$1/2$    cup old fashioned oats

$1/8$    cup flour

$1/4$    cup brown sugar

$1/2$    cup pecans, chopped

$1/4$    cup butter, melted

1. Preheat oven to 350 degrees.
2. Mix apples, cranberries, and sugar together and spread in the bottom of a 9 x 12-inch baking dish.
3. Combine oats, flour, sugar, and pecans in a bowl. Add butter and stir until evenly mixed. Spread over cranberries and apples.
4. Cover with foil and bake for 1 hour. Remove foil and bake another 15 minutes, until brown. Serve hot or cold.

# Apricot Sauce

Pour this over an unfrosted, store-bought cake (nonfat angel food cake or sponge cake, for example) for an exceptionally easy dessert. It's also good over ice cream.

| | |
|---|---|
| 10 | ounces apricot preserves |
| 1/4 | cup sugar |
| 1/4 | cup water |
| 1 | teaspoon lemon juice |

1. Combine all ingredients in a microwavable measuring cup.
2. Microwave for 2 minutes at medium, stirring once.


# Ladyfinger Dessert                                      chill 2 to 3 hours

| | |
|---|---|
| 4 | eggs |
| 8 | teaspoons sugar |
| 8 | ounces semisweet chocolate bits |
| 4 | tablespoons water |
| 2 | teaspoon vanilla |
| 16 | ladyfingers |
| 1/2 | cup whipping cream (optional) |

1. Separate egg yolks from whites. Beat whites until stiff. Beat in 4 teaspoons of the sugar. Set aside. Beat egg yolks and remaining 4 teaspoons of sugar. Set aside.
2. Melt chocolate bits in 4 tablespoons water in double boiler over boiling water. Stir in egg yolks. Cook for 3 minutes.
3. Remove chocolate mixture from heat and fold in egg whites and vanilla.
4. Place 8 ladyfingers in the bottom of a shallow serving dish and cover with half the chocolate mixture. Repeat to make a second layer.
5. Refrigerate for several hours. Serve with whipped cream if desired.

**Yield: 6 to 8 servings**

# Regal Vanilla Pudding

| | |
|---|---|
| 2 | eggs |
| 3/4 | cup sugar |
| 3 | tablespoons cornstarch |
| 3 | cups milk (2% or richer) |
| 1 | tablespoon butter |
| 1 1/2 | teaspoons vanilla |

1. In a small bowl, beat eggs well. Set aside.
2. In a saucepan, combine sugar and cornstarch. Stir in milk.
3. Cook, stirring continuously, over medium heat until mixture thickens and is boiling gently. Remove from heat.
4. Stirring vigorously, add some of the hot mixture to the eggs. Add egg mixture to the saucepan.
5. Cook, stirring slowly, over medium heat until mixture comes close to a boil. Do not boil. Reduce heat to low and continue to cook and stir for 2 minutes more.
6. Remove from heat and stir in butter and vanilla.
7. Pour pudding into dessert dishes or a bowl. Cover tightly with plastic to prevent a skin from forming on the surface and refrigerate.

**Variation**

For a special flavor, add 2 tablespoons brandy or coffee liqueur instead of vanilla.

# Frozen Chocolate Mousse

- 1   cup milk
- 1   envelope unflavored gelatin
- 3/4   cup sugar
- 2   squares unsweetened chocolate
- 2   teaspoons vanilla
- 2   cups heavy cream, softly whipped
-     unsweetened whipped cream (optional)

1. Pour milk into a saucepan and sprinkle with gelatin. Let stand about 5 minutes, until gelatin softens.
2. Warm mixture over medium heat. Add sugar and chocolate and stir continuously until well blended. Do not boil.
3. Remove from heat and let sit until lukewarm. Stir in vanilla and fold in heavy cream.
4. Pour into a mold and freeze until firm. Serve with a dab of unsweetened whipped cream if desired.


# Chocolate Pie

- 3   tablespoons cocoa
- 1   teaspoon flour
- 1 1/4   cups sugar
- 2   eggs
- 1/2   cup evaporated milk
- 1/4   cup butter, melted
- 1   teaspoon vanilla
- 1   pie shell, uncooked
- 1   cup whipping cream

1. Preheat oven to 350 degrees.
2. Mix dry ingredients.
3. In a bowl, beat eggs. Add milk, butter, and vanilla. Combine with dry ingredients
4. Pour into pie shell and bake for 45 minutes.
5. Whip cream and cover the top of the pie when cool. Refrigerate.

# Southern Pecan Tarts

Excellent—and easy.

| | |
|---|---|
| 1/2 | cup butter |
| 1 1/2 | cups pecans, coarsely chopped |
| 1/4 | teaspoon salt |
| 1 | package refrigerated piecrusts |
| 1 | cup corn syrup |
| 1 | cup sugar |
| 1/4 | teaspoon cinnamon |
| 3 | eggs, well beaten |
| 1 | teaspoon vanilla |

1. Preheat oven to 350 degrees.
2. Place 1 tablespoon of the butter on a cookie sheet and melt in preheating oven. Remove.
3. Spread melted butter and pecans on sheet and roast in 350-degree oven for 8 minutes. Remove and sprinkle with salt.
4. On a lightly floured board, roll circles of piecrust with a rolling pin until folds are removed and each is about 1 inch larger all around. Cut small circles from the dough (for minimuffin pans, circles should be about 3 inches in diameter; for regular muffin pans, about 5 inches in diameter). Fit carefully into muffin pans, molding the circles into the cups. The crust should rise above the cup about 1/4 inch.
5. Sprinkle pecans into the tart shells evenly.
6. Stirring constantly, cook the remaining butter in a heavy saucepan until it just starts to brown. Be careful not to burn it. Remove from heat immediately and let cool for 5 minutes.
7. Stir in corn syrup, sugar, cinnamon, eggs, and vanilla. Spoon over the pecans.
8. Bake for 30 to 45 minutes, depending on the size of the muffin pans. Let sit for 10 minutes before removing to a rack to cool.

**Yield: approximately 3 dozen small tarts**

# Pecan Crust

This is a refreshing departure from traditional crusts and good for you as well. Fill it with anything from butterscotch to apple pie for an excellent dessert.

| | |
|---|---|
| ¹⁄₄ | cup sugar |
| 1¹⁄₂ | cups toasted pecans, finely chopped |
| 1 | egg white, slightly beaten |

1. Preheat oven to 350 degrees.
2. Combine sugar and nuts. Stir in egg white and mix well.
3. Spray a pie plate lightly with vegetable oil. Mound nut mixture in the center of the plate. Dampen your hands and pat mixture around the plate and up the sides as evenly as possible.
4. Bake for about 20 minutes. Remove from oven and pat down any puffy areas while hot.

**Variations**

This can be done with any nut or combination of nuts.

# ACCOMPANIMENTS

White Peach and Vidalia Onion Jam
Curry Powder
Herbed Butter Sauce
Herbed Vinegar
Apple Salsa
Dan's Salsa
Cocktail Sauce
Mexican Rub
Herb Rub
Pepper Relish

# White Peach and Vidalia Onion Jam

**Clifton, The Country Inn**
*Rachel Greenberg, Executive Chef*

This recipe is great with pork, lamb, chicken, and tuna. I serve it with a Madeira wine sauce and couscous.

| | |
|---|---|
| ¼ | cup butter |
| 8 | Vidalia onions, diced |
| | salt to taste |
| 6–8 | white peaches |
| | juice of 1 lemon |
| | sugar to taste |
| 2 | tablespoons chopped fresh thyme |

1. Melt butter in a heavy-bottomed, 4-quart saucepan with a tight-fitting lid (the onions should more than half-fill the pan if they are to cook properly).
2. Add onions, turn heat down as low as it will go, and stir in a little salt. Cover. Let cook very slowly, stirring occasionally, as long as 2 hours, until onions are soft and soupy with a little color. Do not let them caramelize. If onions stick or become dry, add 1 cup of water.
3. While onions are cooking, peel and slice peaches. Sprinkle with lemon juice.
4. When onions are done, add peaches to saucepan. Cook for another 5 to 10 minutes over medium heat. Adjust taste with salt and sugar.
5. Add thyme and serve.

**Note**

Feel free to prepare this ahead of time. It keeps well in the refrigerator.

**Variation**

Yellow peaches work equally well. Personally, I prefer a mixture of white and yellow.

# Curry Powder

It is the combinations of spices that make oriental cooking so special. This has a good flavor and saves measuring out a dash of this and a dash of that on busy nights with a dubious outcome. After you try it once, vary it to suit family tastes.

| | |
|---|---|
| 1 | tablespoon ground turmeric |
| 1 | tablespoon ground coriander |
| 1 | teaspoon ground cumin |
| 2 | teaspoons ground peppercorns |
| 1/2 | tablespoon ground ginger |
| 1 | teaspoon ground cardamom |
| 1/2 | teaspoon cayenne |
| 1 | teaspoon ground mace |
| 1 | teaspoon ground cloves |
| 1/2 | teaspoon finely crushed dried rosemary |
| 1/2 | teaspoon finely crushed dried marjoram |
| 1 | teaspoon finely crushed dried basil |
| 1/2 | teaspoon ground fennel |

1. Blend all ingredients in a blender.
2. Store in a small airtight jar.
3. Use as a seasoning in stir-fry and oriental dishes.

# Herbed Butter Sauce

| | |
|---|---|
| 3 | tablespoons white wine vinegar |
| 2 | teaspoons chopped shallots |
| 1 | tablespoon chopped fresh chives |
| 1/4 | cup butter, melted |
| 1 | tablespoon chopped fresh parsley |
| 1/4 | teaspoon dried thyme |

1. Simmer vinegar, shallots, and chives in a saucepan over medium heat until shallots are tender.
2. Add remaining ingredients. Serve with fish.

# Herbed Vinegar

3    **large sprigs each of tarragon, thyme, and rosemary plus additional for garnish**

4    **bay leaves**

$1/4$    **teaspoon fennel seeds**

3    **cups white wine vinegar**

1. Bruise herbs with the back of a spoon or other implement.
2. Pack all ingredients in a jar or bottle with a tight-fitting, non-metallic top. Close bottle tightly and shake well.
3. Store in a cool, dark place and shake daily for 2 to 3 weeks.
4. Strain through cheesecloth.
5. Transfer to smaller bottles with tight-fitting tops, adding a fresh sprig of herb to each if desired.

## Note
These make lovely gifts if you choose attractive bottles.

# Apple Salsa

1    **cup diced, peeled apple**

2    **tablespoons sugar**

$1/2$    **cup red wine**

2    **tablespoons cider vinegar**

2    **tablespoons raisins**

$1/2$    **teaspoon ground ginger**

1. In a saucepan, combine all ingredients and simmer over low heat for 5 to 7 minutes, until slightly thickened.
2. Serve over chicken or pork for a quick and tasty sauce.

# Dan's Salsa

| | |
|---|---|
| 28 | ounces DelMonte diced tomatoes with green peppers and onions |
| 8 | ounces tomato sauce |
| 2–4 | jalapeños, finely diced |
| 2 | tablespoons crushed garlic |
| 1 | yellow bell pepper, diced |
| 1 | cup diced sweet onion |
| 2 | tablespoons chopped fresh oregano |
| 2 | tablespoons chopped fresh cilantro |
| 1 | tablespoon chopped fresh basil |
| 1/4 | cup balsamic vinegar |
| 1/2 | teaspoon ground pepper |
| | salt to taste |

1. Drain tomatoes.
2. Combine all ingredients in a jar or storage container and let sit for several hours.
3. Serve with chips or on vegetables or omelets. Can be stored in the refrigerator for up to a week.

## Note

Chopping by hand makes for a more interesting salsa, but the blender will do very well if you're in a hurry.


# Cocktail Sauce

| | |
|---|---|
| 1/2 | cup catsup |
| 1 | tablespoon diced onion |
| 2 | tablespoons lemon juice |
| 2 | teaspoons horseradish |
| 1 | teaspoon Worcestershire sauce |
| 2 | drops Tabasco |

1. Combine all ingredients.
2. Chill at least 1 hour before serving.

# Mexican Rub

| ¼ | cup chili powder |
|---|---|
| 1 | tablespoon onion powder |
| 1 | tablespoon cumin |
| 2 | teaspoons salt |
| 1½ | teaspoons dried oregano |
| 1 | teaspoon garlic powder |
| 1 | teaspoon ground red pepper |

1. Combine all ingredients.
2. Store in an airtight container for use on poultry, beef, and fish.

# Herb Rub

| 1 | tablespoon dried thyme |
|---|---|
| 1 | tablespoon dried oregano |
| 1½ | teaspoons poultry seasoning |
| 1 | teaspoon dried rosemary |
| 1 | teaspoon dried marjoram |
| 1 | teaspoon dried basil |
| 1 | teaspoon dried parsley flakes |
| ½ | teaspoon salt |
| ¼ | teaspoon pepper |

1. Combine all ingredients.
2. Store in an airtight container for use on chicken, pork, or fish.

---

*These mountains are the Eden of the United States.*

**—Thomas Jefferson**, 1797

# Pepper Relish

This recipe has been in my family for generations and produces the very best relish. Make it in September, when peppers are cheap, and you'll have a lovely Christmas or house gift. With the red and green of the peppers, the jars look beautiful.

| | |
|---|---|
| 1 | quart chopped red peppers ($\frac{1}{4}$-inch or smaller; see note) |
| 1$\frac{1}{2}$ | quarts chopped green peppers ($\frac{1}{4}$-inch or smaller) |
| 2$\frac{1}{2}$ | quarts chopped yellow onions ($\frac{1}{4}$-inch or smaller) |
| 2 | jalapeños, chopped into $\frac{1}{4}$-inch pieces (optional) |
| 3–4 | quarts boiling water |
| 1 | quart vinegar |
| 2$\frac{1}{2}$ | tablespoons salt |
| 3 | cups sugar |

1. Place peppers and onions in a large pot. Pour boiling water over to cover. Let stand 5 minutes.
2. Drain in a colander.
3. Return to pot and pour more boiling water over to cover. Let stand 10 minutes. Drain well, for 10 to 15 minutes.
4. Return to pot and add vinegar, salt, and sugar. Cook for 15 minutes over medium heat.
5. Fill hot, sterile jars with hot mixture and seal.

**Yield: 7 to 9 pints**

**Notes**

The food processor works best for chopping the peppers and onions.

Be sure to sterilize the cup used to fill the jars and the lids as well as the jars.

When pickling things for preservation, use vinegar with 4 to 6 percent acidity (vinegars are labeled with their acidity). I use plain cider vinegar for this.

**Variations**

You can vary the quantities of fruit, but the amounts of onions and peppers should be roughly equal. Be sure to keep the same proportion of vinegar, salt, and sugar.

# INDEX